Theory Test Made Easy

The step-by-step guide to help
you pass the Theory Test

Published by AA Publishing (a trading name of AA Media Ltd, whose registered office is Grove House, Chineham Court, Basingstoke, Hampshire RG24 8AG; registered number 06112600).

First aid information on pages 112–113 reproduced from The Official Highway Code, Department for Transport and Driver and Vehicle Standards Agency © Crown Copyright 2022. Contains public sector information licensed under the Open Government Licence v3.0.

Images on pages 15 and 16 reproduced under licence from the Driver and Vehicle Standards Agency.

Road signs are reproduced under the terms of the Open Government Licence.

Written by Jane Gregory
Consultants: Sue Hubbard, Ruth Johnson and Keith Bell

ISBN: 978-0-7495-8309-5

Printed and bound in the UK by Bell & Bain Ltd

A05828

CONTENTS

Save £40
on your first 10 lessons*
theaa.com/driving-school

AA Driving School

About the theory test

The driving test has two parts: the theory test (which includes multiple-choice questions and the hazard perception test) and the practical driving test.

- The theory test is all about making you a safer driver.

- It is easier to understand the theory test if you are putting your learning into practice – that is, having lessons in practical driving at the same time as getting ready to take your theory test.

Using this book

This book is designed to help you tackle the questions in the theory test part of the driving test.

- Each chapter covers the same topic as the *AA Theory Test for Car Drivers*, which you should refer to as it contains all the latest revision questions from the Driver and Vehicle Standards Agency (DVSA).

- The chapters include information to help you understand the topic and the questions, as well as sample questions for practice.

- You will also need a copy of *The Highway Code*.

Applying for a theory test

- Find out where your nearest theory test centre is by asking your driving instructor. You can also call the Driver and Vehicle Standards Agency (DVSA) on 0300 200 1122 or visit gov.uk/book-theory-test.

- You should get a date and time in about two weeks, though it might be a little longer if you are a driver with special needs. Some centres have appointments on Saturdays and at weekends as well as in the week.

- When you book you should have ready your **provisional licence** and a **credit or debit card** (the person who books the test must be the cardholder, or the cardholder must be present). Application forms are available online and from Approved Driving Instructors (ADIs). Check gov.uk for the current fee.

Common questions

Q. What are the questions in the theory test like?

- At the test centre, you will sit at a computer with the theory test questions loaded on it. Remember there are two parts to the theory test: multiple-choice questions and the hazard perception test.

- The questions will be based on similar topics in each of the chapters in this book.

- All the questions have a number of answers and you **touch the answer** you have chosen on the computer screen or use the mouse to click.

Q. How many answers are there for each question?

- The theory test for car drivers will always ask you to choose one answer from four options. The computer will alert you if you have not selected an answer.

Q. Will the computer be easy to use?

- Only one question appears on the screen at a time, and they are easy to read.

Q. I am dyslexic, so I read slowly. Can I have extra time?

- Candidates with dyslexia can take their theory test with an English or Welsh language voiceover. Check with the DVSA for details.

Q. English is not my first language. Can I do the theory test in any language?

- Candidates can only take the test in English or Welsh. They cannot take the test using a foreign language voiceover or interpreter.

Q. When will I know if I have passed the theory test?

- You will be told straight away, before you leave the theory test centre, so you won't have to wait for a letter or phone call. Remember – keep your theory test pass certificate safe, because you will have to take it with you when you take your practical driving test.

What to expect of the multiple-choice questions

- The multiple-choice questions have four possible answers listed after the question. You have to choose the one answer you think is correct.

- You will have **57 minutes** to do **50 questions**. You have to get at least **43 right** to pass this part of the theory test.

- Five of the 50 questions will be **case studies** (see pages 8–10).

- You can move backwards and forwards through the questions and 'flag' any that you want to go back to later. You can also change your answer if you need to. But you can't do this in the hazard perception part of the test.

- After you have done this part of the test, you will get a short break of about three to five minutes. Then you will go on to do the hazard perception part of the test.

Case study questions

Typically, five of the 50 questions will take the form of a case study. All five questions will be based on a single driving situation and appear one at time.

Q. What's a case study?

Case studies are driving situations you might find yourself in. Just as with the other questions, put yourself in the position of the driver who needs to make a decision.

Q. Does it work in the same way as the other questions?

Yes. There may be a little more text to read through, but don't worry as this is setting the scene for the question.

The case study in your theory test could be based on any driving scenario and ask questions from a range of topics in the DVSA's live database of questions.

The sample case study on the following pages demonstrates how the case study questions may appear in your live test, so you'll know what to expect.

See page 10 for the answers.

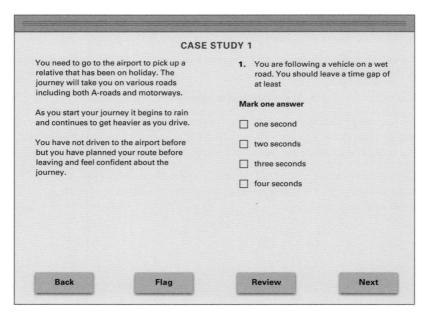

CASE STUDY 1

You need to go to the airport to pick up a relative that has been on holiday. The journey will take you on various roads including both A-roads and motorways.

As you start your journey it begins to rain and continues to get heavier as you drive.

You have not driven to the airport before but you have planned your route before leaving and feel confident about the journey.

1. You are following a vehicle on a wet road. You should leave a time gap of at least

Mark one answer

☐ one second

☐ two seconds

☐ three seconds

☐ four seconds

| Back | Flag | Review | Next |

CASE STUDY 1

You need to go to the airport to pick up a relative that has been on holiday. The journey will take you on various roads including both A-roads and motorways.

As you start your journey it begins to rain and continues to get heavier as you drive.

You have not driven to the airport before but you have planned your route before leaving and feel confident about the journey.

2. What does this sign mean?

Mark one answer

- ☐ you have priority
- ☐ no motor vehicles
- ☐ two-way traffic
- ☐ no overtaking

| Back | Flag | Review | Next |

CASE STUDY 1

You need to go to the airport to pick up a relative that has been on holiday. The journey will take you on various roads including both A-roads and motorways.

As you start your journey it begins to rain and continues to get heavier as you drive.

You have not driven to the airport before but you have planned your route before leaving and feel confident about the journey.

3. You have just gone through deep water. To dry off the brakes you should

Mark one answer

- ☐ accelerate and keep to a high speed for a short time
- ☐ go slowly while gently applying the brakes
- ☐ avoid using the brakes at all for a few miles
- ☐ stop for at least an hour to allow them time to dry

| Back | Flag | Review | Next |

CASE STUDY 1

You need to go to the airport to pick up a relative that has been on holiday. The journey will take you on various roads including both A-roads and motorways.

As you start your journey it begins to rain and continues to get heavier as you drive.

You have not driven to the airport before but you have planned your route before leaving and feel confident about the journey.

4. A bus has stopped at a bus stop ahead of you. Its right-hand indicator is flashing. You should

Mark one answer

☐ flash your headlights and slow down

☐ slow down and give way if it is safe to do so

☐ sound your horn and keep going

☐ slow down and then sound your horn

Back   Flag   Review   Next

CASE STUDY 1

You need to go to the airport to pick up a relative that has been on holiday. The journey will take you on various roads including both A-roads and motorways.

As you start your journey it begins to rain and continues to get heavier as you drive.

You have not driven to the airport before but you have planned your route before leaving and feel confident about the journey.

5. Where you see street lights but no speed limit signs the limit is usually

Mark one answer

☐ 30mph

☐ 40mph

☐ 50mph

☐ 60mph

Back   Flag   Review   Next

Answers to sample case study questions:

1D 2D 3B 4B 5A

SOME 'DOs' AND 'DON'Ts'

DO   prepare for the theory test as part of a full course of driving lessons with an instructor from a reputable driving school. Fully qualified driving instructors are called Approved Driving Instructors (ADIs, see page 14).

DON'T   take the theory test before you start practical lessons. You will learn to be a safe driver if you have practical lessons first. Then, studying for the theory test will make more sense to you.

DO   buy an up-to-date book with the questions in it to help you prepare for the theory test. The *AA Theory Test for Car Drivers* book has all the revision questions and answers. It will help you get used to the types of questions that are in the test. It will also help you recognise the key words that come up in the questions.

DON'T   try to learn all the questions. There are far too many (more than 700) and the questions on an actual test will be different from the questions published in revision books, although they will cover the same topics. The aim of the theory test is to make sure you really understand about driving and safety before you get your full licence to drive.

Always keep a copy of *The Highway Code* handy and read a few pages when you have a spare minute. If you know the Highway Code it will help you answer the theory test questions.

Hints and tips for answering multiple-choice questions

1. **Don't panic.** Maybe you hate exams. Maybe it's a long time since you took an exam. You can still pass the theory test if you prepare well, with help from your driving instructor.

2. Look at **one question at a time** and try to answer it. Don't read them all at once.

3. **Read the question first** and decide what **you** think the right answer is.

4. If there are any **pictures or diagrams** with the question, study them carefully – they should give you some clues about the right answer.

5. **Read through the answers** and choose the one that seems closest to the answer you had decided on yourself.

If you approach each question like this, you will avoid being confused by answers with similar wording.

What to expect in the hazard perception test

- The hazard perception test helps to make sure that new drivers know all about hazards and how to look out for them before they are allowed to drive on their own.

- Learner drivers need more training in how to spot hazards, because they are often so busy thinking about using the car's controls that they forget to watch the road and traffic.

- Proper training can really help you to see more of the hazards you will meet when driving, and to see those hazards earlier.

- New drivers have just had lessons, so they should remember how to drive safely. But in fact new drivers have most accidents.

Q. What is hazard perception?

- A hazard is anything that might cause you to change speed or direction when driving.

- The aim of the hazard perception test is to find out how good you are at noticing hazards coming up on the road ahead.

- The test will also show how much you know about the risks of driving. That is:
  – risks to you as a driver
  – risks to your passengers
  – and risks to other road users.

Q. What happens in the hazard perception test?

- The hazard perception test follows the multiple-choice part of the test. It contains 14 clips from the perspective of a driver and lasts about 20 minutes.

- First, there is a short introduction explaining how the test works. You will also get a chance to practise with the computer and mouse control before you start the test for real. This is to make sure you know what to expect, and that you are happy with what you have to do.

TWO IMPORTANT POINTS

1. As you have to learn about hazard perception before you take the theory test, it is important to have lessons with a **qualified driving instructor from a good driving school.**

A qualified instructor is called an ADI. ADI stands for Approved Driving Instructor. It means they have studied and taken a special test themselves. Look for the green ADI certificate on the windscreen of their car.

2. You should **not take your theory test too early**. This is because you need the experience of meeting real hazards while you are learning to drive, so that you will be able to pass the hazard perception part of the theory test.

You must pass the theory test before you can take the practical driving test. Agree a plan of action with your driving instructor.

Q. Do I touch the screen when I see a hazard on the screen?

- As soon as you see a hazard coming up, you **click the mouse** control.

Q. Will I have enough time to see the hazard before the picture changes?

- Don't worry, you will have plenty of time to see the hazard – but the sooner you notice it, the more marks you will score.

Q. What are the hazard perceptions clips like?

- You will see video clips of a street scene with traffic such as cars, pedestrians, cyclists, etc. The scenes are presented from the point of view of a driver in a car. You will see 14 video clips.

- You have to notice **hazards that are developing** on the road ahead — that is, problems building up that could lead to an accident.

Q. How many hazards are in each clip?

- Every clip has **at least one hazard** in it — one clip will have two hazards.

Q. How many hazards do I have to spot altogether?

- You should find **15 hazards** to 'click' on during the 20 minutes.

Q. Can I go back and change my mind?

- Each test clip will be shown only once, so you must concentrate. You cannot go back to an earlier clip and change your response.

Q. *How is the test scored?*

- For each hazard you spot you get one or more points.

- You get more or less points depending on how quickly you spot the hazard developing on-screen, and click on it with the mouse. If you see the potential hazard too late, you may not score anything at all.

- You have to score a minimum of **44 out of 75 to pass** this element of the theory test.

Q. *What stops me from clicking all the time?*

- The computer has checks built in to show up anyone trying to cheat – for example, someone who keeps clicking the mouse all the time. You may see a warning screen similar to the one below if the computer detects a clicking pattern or you click the mouse constantly.

You responded to this clip
in an unacceptable manner.
You will score zero
for this clip.

Pass or Fail

Remember, you have to pass **both** the **multiple-choice section and the hazard perception** part of the theory test to get a pass. At the end of the test they will tell you your scores for both parts. If you didn't pass, this will help you see where you need to do better next time.

A practice run

You won't be able to practice with the real clips used in the test.

This is because the whole idea of the hazard perception element of the theory test is to see **how fast you can spot** and **react to hazards**. If you had seen the actual clips before, it would not be a realistic or useful test.

Q. So how can I practice?

- ADIs have **training books and software** to work through with you during your driving lessons.

- There are some **practice clips** on www.gov.uk to help you.

How your instructor can help

Your driving instructor has been trained to help you learn hazard perception skills, and can give you plenty of practice in:

- what to look out for when driving

- how to anticipate (be ready for) hazards

- what action to take when you have to deal with hazards of all kinds.

How to prepare yourself for the test

You may be worried about the exam feel of the theory test. Try **not** to worry about this, because:

- The people at the test centre will do their best to put you at your ease.
- The computer is easy to use.
- You are doing this for yourself, not for anyone else.
- You will be told the results of your test before you leave the theory test centre.

All you have to do to pass the theory test is:
1. Have lessons with a **reputable driving school**
2. Know **The Highway Code**.

Feeling okay on the day

Do whatever you know will make you feel most relaxed – go for a walk in the fresh air or listen to some music. For obvious reasons, this is not the time to drink alcohol.

Just before you start the test, take a few deep breaths so that you feel calm, and then begin working steadily through the questions – one at a time.

Good luck!

1. ALERTNESS

The first section in the theory test question books is headed 'Alertness'. It is a short section, so it's a good choice for your first attempt at dealing with the questions

Q. What does it mean to be alert?

- Alertness means: being wide awake and concentrating on your driving.

- Alertness means: looking out for hazards.

- Alertness means: noticing all road signs and road markings, and acting on the instructions they give.

Tackling the questions

Look at the questions in the **Alertness** section of your theory test book. See if you can pick out the **key word** in each question.

You'll see that the **Alertness** questions are about:

- anticipation
- observation
- signalling
- reversing
- using your mirrors
- concentration
- getting distracted
- feeling sleepy
- using mobile phones.

Sample questions and explanations

In the pages that follow, we shall look at some sample questions similar to the ones you will get in the real test.

Each question is followed by an explanation to show you why the right answer is the right answer.

We'll also give you extra information about the topic to help you while you are learning to drive.

Note: You'll find more questions that deal with the topics listed above when you get to the section on 'Hazard awareness' (Chapter 5, pages 51–62), which covers things that might make you feel less alert.

Sample questions – Alertness

SAMPLE QUESTION 1

If you are driving behind a long vehicle you should keep well back. Why is this?

Mark one answer

- ☐ **A.** It leaves you more room if you want to take a corner quickly
- ☐ **B.** It allows the driver to see you in their mirrors
- ☐ **C.** It shields you from the wind
- ☐ **D.** It leaves room for another car to cut in behind the long vehicle

Working out the answer to question 1

To work out the right answer, look at the question first and decide what you think the answer is. Then see if any of those given (**A, B, C** or **D**) fits the answer you have thought of yourself.

Look at the answers in turn:

Answer A   This answer is saying that the reason for holding back is to give you room to turn a corner at speed.

You know from your driving lessons that you should never take a corner too quickly.

Therefore, **answer A** can't be the right answer.

Answer B   If you are driving too close to a long vehicle, you are hidden from the driver by the vehicle itself. If the driver can see you in their mirrors they will know where you are when they plan to slow down or change direction, and will see if you signal to overtake.

So **answer B** does not seem to have anything wrong with it – it could be the one to choose.

Answer C   Being shielded from the wind is not a key driving skill. Also, **common sense** tells you that **answer C** cannot be right. Obviously if you are well back you are *less* shielded from the wind. Also, you know that it is not a good idea to drive close behind a long vehicle for *any* reason, as long vehicles need more time and space to stop or change direction than smaller vehicles.

Answer D   It is true that if you are keeping a safe distance behind the long vehicle, this may leave space for another vehicle to cut in and fill the gap. However, that would be bad driving on their part, so this can't be the right answer either.

So B is the right answer.

Question 1 was about being **alert** and **anticipating** that a long vehicle may need more room.

Now try one about using your skills of **alertness** and **observation**.

SAMPLE QUESTION 2

You are driving on a dual carriageway and see a white arrow painted on the centre of the road, curving to the left. What does it mean?

Mark one answer

- ☐ **A.** Drivers must move on to the hard shoulder
- ☐ **B.** It tells overtaking drivers there is a bend to the left
- ☐ **C.** Overtaking drivers must move back to the left
- ☐ **D.** It is safe to overtake

Working out the answer to question 2

This question seems to have something to do with **overtaking**, as that word comes into three of the answers. However, it doesn't come into **answer A;** could that answer be right?

Answer A   The clue to this is in the first part of the sentence – 'You are driving on a dual carriageway'.

A hard shoulder is normally found only on a motorway. And the instruction telling motorists to use the hard shoulder is a large sign high above the carriageway, not a white arrow painted on the road.

So **answer A** must be wrong.

Answer B   Check the signs in *The Highway Code* and you will see that the road sign for a left-hand bend is a black boomerang-shape inside a red triangle.

It's a sign displayed on a pole, not a road marking. So **answer B** must be wrong too.

(By the way – do you know what the sign is for 'No left turn'? If you're not sure, look that up in *The Highway Code* as well.)

Answer C   A white arrow painted on the road and curving to the left indicates that it's not safe to overtake after that point.

It's a warning to any drivers still overtaking that they should return to the normal road position as soon as they can do so safely.

Answer D   The white arrow is pointing left, to guide you back to the normal road position because it's not safe to overtake. So **answer D** is wrong.

So C is the right answer.

The last two sample questions in this chapter are about **concentrating** and **not being distracted** while you are driving.

Other sections cover feeling sleepy while driving, and losing concentration due to drink or drugs.

Did you know?

The main causes of distraction are:

- loud music in the car
- passengers (usually children)
- events happening outside (such as accidents)
- using a mobile phone while driving

SAMPLE QUESTION 3

You have some lucky dice hanging from your interior mirror. They may

Mark one answer

- [ ] **A.** restrict your view
- [ ] **B.** help you drive better
- [ ] **C.** keep you better focussed
- [ ] **D.** help you to concentrate on your driving

Working out the answer to question 3

Answer A   The interior mirror is the one inside the car – often called the rear-view mirror.

It stands to reason you need to see as much as possible of the road and traffic around you through your windscreen and in your mirrors so that you can spot hazards. So anything that gets in the way and blocks (restricts) your view is a bad idea.

So **answer A** could be the right answer.

Answer B   Perhaps if they are 'lucky' dice you think they will help you drive better? But common sense tells that you that **answer B** is wrong.

Answer C   This is obviously wrong as you should be looking at the road rather than the dice.

Answer D   It's hard to see how something moving about in front of you can help you concentrate; it's much more likely to put you off. So **answer D** is wrong.

So A is the right answer.

SAMPLE QUESTION 4

If your mobile phone rings while you are on a journey you should

Mark one answer

☐ **A.** stop the car immediately

☐ **B.** answer it immediately

☐ **C.** find a safe place, pull up, and then answer it

☐ **D.** find a kerb and pull up next to it

Working out the answer to question 4

Answer A You would never stop the car immediately just to take a phone call. You have to find a safe place to stop first. Imagine if you were on the outside lane of a motorway – you certainly could not 'stop immediately'. So **answer A** must be wrong.

Answer B You should never make calls on your mobile phone while on the move. You should not answer them on the move either. So **answer B** is wrong.

The best thing is to wait till you can **find a safe place to stop and then deal with the call.**

Better still: make use of **voicemail** so that the caller can leave a message on your phone and you can call back at a time when you are not driving.

Answer C Look at the explanation above; **answer C** sounds like this, so is likely to be right.

Answer D The important thing to do is to find a *safe* place to pull up. A kerb is not always more safe than, say, a lay-by, or a quiet side road. So **answer D** is wrong.

So C is the right answer.

2. ATTITUDE

Attitude is a very important part of being a good driver. Your attitude when you are driving plays a big part in ensuring your safety and that of other road users.

Q. What is meant by attitude?

- Attitude means: your frame of mind when you get into the car.

- Attitude means: how you react when you meet hazards on the road.

- Attitude means: whether you lose patience or stay calm.

- Attitude means: how you behave towards other drivers.

Think about these two sentences:

1. I aim to be a careful and safe driver.

2. I aim to be a fast and skilful driver.

Does the first one sound boring to you?
Does the second one sound much more fun?

What is your attitude to the rules of the road?

Some people think:

- that speed limits are only meant for people who can't react to hazards quickly.

- that 'no overtaking' rules are only meant for people who don't have powerful cars.

Attitudes like these explain why accidents that could be avoided, still happen.

If you don't want to end up as 'just another statistic', **being a safe and careful driver is the only way to go.**

A car is a powerful thing

People often don't realise what a powerful weapon they are in control of when they get behind the wheel of a car.

Think about whether you would ever use your car to fight a battle with another driver.

You only have to think about this to understand how important attitude is in driving.

Defensive driving is good driving

Q. What does 'defensive driving' mean?

- anticipating hazards

- showing consideration to other road users

- not taking risks.

Look up the theory test questions that come under the heading of **Attitude.** You'll see that they cover many of the points in the **DOs** and **DON'Ts** on the next page, such as:

- tailgating

- consideration for other road users, including pedestrians, buses, slow-moving vehicles and horse riders

- driving at the right speed for the conditions

- when to flash headlights.

Did you know?

People aged 19 and under driving in their first six months have the highest annual accident rates.

Here is a list of DOs and DON'Ts for good drivers

Good drivers do –

✓ drive at the right speed for the road and traffic conditions

✓ observe speed limits

✓ overtake only when it is safe to do so

✓ park in correct and safe places

✓ wait patiently if the driver in front is not sure of the way, or is a learner

✓ look out for vulnerable road users such as cyclists

✓ concentrate on their driving at all times

✓ plan their journeys so that they have plenty of time to get to their destination.

Good drivers don't –

✗ allow themselves to get involved in 'road rage'

✗ break speed limits

✗ drive too fast in wet, icy or foggy weather

✗ accelerate or brake too harshly

✗ overtake and 'cut in', forcing others to brake sharply

✗ put pressure on other drivers by coming up too close behind them (this is called tailgating), flashing headlights, etc

✗ allow their attention to be distracted by passengers, mobile phones or loud music.

Sample questions – Attitude

SAMPLE QUESTION 5

What does 'tailgating' mean?

Mark one answer

- [ ] **A.** Driving while using rear fog lights
- [ ] **B.** Reversing into a parking space
- [ ] **C.** Following too closely behind the vehicle in front
- [ ] **D.** Getting out of a hatchback via the rear door

Working out the answer to question 5

As you have probably realised by now, usually one of the four answers makes no sense at all. In this case, it's **answer D.** So you can cross that one off the list straight away.

If you know *The Highway Code*, you can also cross off answers **A** and **B,** because you know that tailgating means **following too closely behind the vehicle in front**.

So C is the right answer.

Q. Why is tailgating dangerous?

- A large number of accidents are caused by **rear-end shunts** – where the vehicle behind crashes into the one in front.

- As well as the risks to life and health, this kind of accident can be very costly, because *the driver behind is nearly always in the wrong and has to pay.*

- You should always leave enough space between your vehicle and the one in front, so that you can stop safely if the driver in front suddenly slows down or stops (see Safety Margins, pages 39–50).

SAMPLE QUESTION 6

You are driving at the right speed for the road you are on, but a driver behind is trying to overtake you. What should you do?

Mark one answer

☐ **A.** Move into the middle of the road to stop them overtaking

☐ **B.** Move nearer to the car in front so they have no room to overtake

☐ **C.** Signal left and wave them on so they can overtake

☐ **D.** Carry on driving at the speed limit but increase the gap slightly between your vehicle and the one in front

Working out the answer to question 6

If you are driving at the right speed and in the right position on the road, there is **no need to change what you are doing**. But pull back a bit from the vehicle in front so if the driver behind insists on overtaking, there is less risk of an accident.

Do not try to stop the car behind from overtaking. Do not move into the middle of the road or move up close to the car in front. These actions could be very dangerous.

You should not give **confusing signals** such as indicating left or waving the other driver on.

So D is the right answer.

Did you know?

If you break the law and collect **six or more penalty points** on your licence in the two years after you pass your test, you'll **lose your licence** and have to start again as a learner.

3. SAFETY AND YOUR VEHICLE

Go to your book of theory test questions and look through the section headed 'Safety and your vehicle'.

You will notice that the questions in this section are a bit of a mixture. They cover many topics about safety, including:

- understanding the controls of your vehicle
- what the car's warning lights tell you
- tyres – correct inflation, pressures and tread depths
- when to switch on hazard warning lights
- passenger safety
- the environment
- security and crime prevention.

Now try going through the section again and see if you can put the questions into groups.

- Which ones belong under which of the headings above?
- How many questions can you find that are about helping the environment?

Sample questions – Safety and your vehicle

Remember that questions on the same topic may appear in more than one section; so, if we don't cover the topic here, it will probably be covered later on in this book.

SAMPLE QUESTION 7

For which of the following reasons may you switch on hazard warning lights?

Mark one answer

- [ ] **A.** You need to double-park for a short time
- [ ] **B.** You need to park on double yellow lines
- [ ] **C.** You are being towed
- [ ] **D.** You have broken down

Working out the answer to question 7

Double-parking means parking your vehicle in the road beside another parked car.

You know from *The Highway Code* that you are not allowed to **double-park** – even for a short time. So the answer cannot be **A**.

In some circumstances you may **stop** on **double yellow lines** (for example, to load or unload goods), but you must not **park** on double yellow lines. So **B** is also wrong.

Look up all the sections that deal with **parking rules** in *The Highway Code*. Find out the rules for **red routes, white lines** and **zigzag lines** as well as yellow lines.

What about answer C?

The rule is, you should never switch on your hazard warning lights while your vehicle is moving. There is only one exception to this rule, and it applies when you are approaching slow or stopped traffic on a motorway. So **C** is wrong.

Hazard warning lights are just that; they warn other road users of a hazard ahead. So you would need to switch on your hazard warning lights if **you have broken down** and your vehicle is causing an obstruction.

So D is the right answer.

SAMPLE QUESTION 8

What is the legal minimum tread depth for car tyres over three-quarters of the breadth?

Mark one answer

☐ **A.** 1mm

☐ **B.** 1.6mm

☐ **C.** 2.5mm

☐ **D.** 4mm

Working out the answer to question 8

This is one of the more straightforward questions in the theory test, because you either know the answer, or you don't!

If you have studied *The Highway Code* you'll know that **B** is the right answer – tyres must have a depth of tread of 1.6 millimetres for at least three-quarters of the width of the tyre ('breadth' is another word for 'width'). This is a **legal** requirement; that means, it's the law.

Note: If you're not sure what 1.6mm looks like, make time to check.

SAMPLE QUESTION 9

You have two young teenagers as passengers in your car. Who is responsible for their safety? Is it

Mark one answer

☐   **A.** you, the driver

☐   **B.** the parents of the teenagers

☐   **C.** the teenagers, because they are old enough to look after themselves

☐   **D.** any other adult travelling with you

Working out the answer to question 9

You can see that **answer D** does not make sense, because there may not be another adult with you.

You might think that older children can look after themselves – but the law doesn't see it that way. **Answer C** is wrong too.

As for **answer B**, even if the parents of the teenagers have asked you to give them a lift, you are still responsible for their safety. As the driver, you are always responsible by law for the safety of everyone travelling in your car.

So A is the right answer.

If any of your passengers are young people under 14, you are responsible for making sure they are wearing seat belts. You are responsible for them by law **even if you are a learner driver yourself.**

SAMPLE QUESTION 10

On what part of your vehicle would you expect to find a catalytic converter?

Mark one answer

- ☐ **A.** The fuel tank
- ☐ **B.** The air filter
- ☐ **C.** The exhaust system
- ☐ **D.** The cooling system

Working out the answer to question 10

To answer this, you need to know that cars are fitted with **catalytic converters** to reduce **exhaust emissions**.

Exhaust emissions are the poisonous gases that come out of the vehicle's exhaust and can **harm both people and the environment.** The catalytic converter (or 'cat') will work to make those exhaust fumes cleaner.

Designers of new cars are working all the time on cleaner systems that do less harm to the environment.

So C is the right answer.

A CONFUSING QUESTION

One question in particular seems to cause problems for many learner drivers.

The question goes something like:

What kind of driving results in high fuel consumption?

The answer of course is **bad** driving – especially harsh braking and acceleration. This means that you will use more fuel; and 'high fuel consumption' means using more fuel than you should.

But many people read the word **'high'** as meaning **'good'** – as in 'a high level of driving skill' – and so they end up picking the wrong answer.

And more confusion...

The second most confusing question is the one about **braking distances** and **stopping distances**.

Always remember that:
the stopping distance = the thinking distance + the braking distance.

For help with this, see the next chapter, which is about safety margins.

If you find some words in the questions confusing, look them up in the **Glossary** section at the back of this book.

4. SAFETY MARGINS

A safety margin is the space you need to leave between your vehicle and the one in front so that you will not crash into it if it slows down or stops suddenly.

- Experienced drivers are usually better than new or learner drivers at leaving good safety margins. Learner drivers find it harder to keep their vehicle at a safe distance from the one in front.

In this chapter we will look in more detail at what The Highway Code has to say about:

- safe stopping distances
- safe separation distances (these are the same as safety margins).

Safety margins

In *The Highway Code* these are called 'Separation Distances' or 'Stopping Distances'. Look them up in the index at the back of *The Highway Code* and find the pages that refer to them. Also look at the table on page 43 of this book.

IMPORTANT NOTE

Any driver can feel pressured to speed up by drivers behind them.

Don't let other drivers make you cut down on your safety margins. Stay a safe distance behind the vehicle in front. Then you will have enough time to anticipate, and react to, hazards.

The two-second rule
In traffic that's moving at normal speed, allow at least a two-second gap between you and the vehicle in front.

Safe stopping distances

People who are taking their theory test often get confused about this.

- Look through the Safety Margins section of your book of theory test questions.

- Notice that some of them ask you about your **overall stopping distance**.

Q. What is meant by overall stopping distance?

- **Overall stopping distance** or **stopping distance** is not the same as **braking distance**.

- **Stopping distance** is made up of: **thinking distance + braking distance.**

- In other words, the time it takes to notice that there's a hazard ahead plus the time it takes to brake to deal with it.

Here's an example:

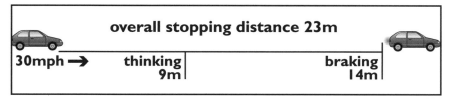

overall stopping distance 23m

30mph → | thinking 9m | braking 14m

Thinking distance is sometimes called **reaction time** or **reaction distance**. If you are driving at 30mph, your thinking distance will be 9 metres (30 feet). That means your vehicle will travel 9 metres or 30 feet **before you start braking**.

Q. What is the link between stopping distance and safety margins?

- You should always **leave enough space** between your vehicle and the one in front. If the other driver has to slow down suddenly or stop without warning, you need to be able to stop safely.

This **space** is your **safety margin**.

Safety margins for other vehicles

- **Long vehicles and motorcycles need more room to stop** – in other words, you must leave a **bigger safety margin** when following a long vehicle or a motorbike.

- When driving behind a long vehicle, **pull back** to increase your distance and your safety margin so that you get a better view of the road ahead – there could be hazards developing.

- Strong winds can blow lorries and motorbikes off course, so leave a **bigger safety margin**.

Did you know?

Motorbike riders are **vulnerable road users**. In an accident, a biker can be in **more danger** than a car driver. A biker could be thrown on to the road and then be run over by the car behind.

The basic road safety rule here is:
don't get closer than the overall stopping distance.

Look at the diagram on the next page and learn the stopping distances at various speeds.

STOPPING DISTANCES

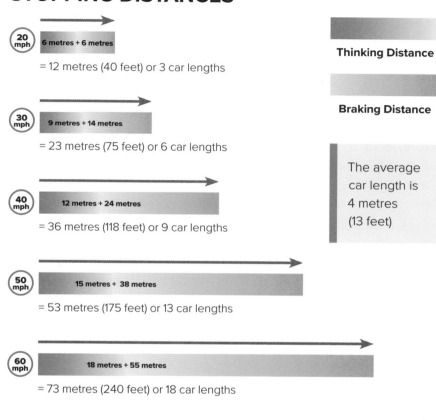

20 mph

6 metres + 6 metres

= 12 metres (40 feet) or 3 car lengths

30 mph

9 metres + 14 metres

= 23 metres (75 feet) or 6 car lengths

40 mph

12 metres + 24 metres

= 36 metres (118 feet) or 9 car lengths

50 mph

15 metres + 38 metres

= 53 metres (175 feet) or 13 car lengths

60 mph

18 metres + 55 metres

= 73 metres (240 feet) or 18 car lengths

70 mph

21 metres + 75 metres

= 96 metres (315 feet) or 24 car lengths

Thinking Distance

Braking Distance

The average
car length is
4 metres
(13 feet)

Note: It's better to learn this table than to have to
learn by your mistakes. Don't let your experience
of near-misses teach you about safety margins the
hard way.

Different conditions and safety margins

One or more questions in your theory test might be about driving in 'different conditions'. These questions aim to make sure you know what **adjustments** (changes) you should make to your driving when either:

road conditions are different from normal (for example, when parts of the road are closed off for roadworks)

or weather conditions affect your driving.

Roadworks

You should always take extra care when you see a sign warning you that there are roadworks ahead.

Remember, roadworks are a *hazard* and you have to *anticipate* what to do.

If you see the driver ahead slowing down, take this as a sign that you should do the same – even if you can't see a hazard ahead. You still need to keep a safe distance from the car in front.

Harassing the driver in front by tailgating is both wrong and dangerous. So is *overtaking* to fill the gap.

Roadworks on motorways

It's especially important that you know what to do when you see a sign for roadworks ahead on a motorway.

- There may be a **lower speed limit** than normal – keep to it.

- Use your **mirrors** and **indicators**, and get into the **correct lane** in plenty of time.

- **Don't overtake** the queue and then force your way in at the last minute (this is an example of showing an inconsiderate **attitude** to other road users).

- Always keep a **safe distance** from the vehicle in front.

Weather conditions

In bad weather (often referred to as 'adverse' weather) you need to increase your safety margins.

Look again at the two-second rule on page 40. When it's raining, you need to leave at **least twice as much room** between you and the vehicle in front. When there's ice on the road, leave an even bigger gap.

When it's icy you should multiply your two-second gap by ten.

In adverse weather, motorways may lower advised speed limits. You should always obey the signs, and not let yourself be pressured by other people into **driving too fast for the conditions**.

How adverse weather conditions are covered in *The Highway Code* and the theory test

You will find information on driving in adverse weather conditions in *The Highway Code*. Look these rules up and read through them, perhaps learning two or three at a time.

Now look up the section headed Vehicle Handling in your book of theory test questions. You'll see that there are many questions about driving in bad weather in this section, too.

There are questions on two other topics in Safety Margins:

- questions on **how to control your vehicle**, especially on downhill slopes
- questions about **anti-lock brakes.**

Controlling your vehicle

Ask your driving instructor about what you should do when you reach a steep downhill slope. What **gear** should you use? What does **engine braking** mean?

Anti-lock brakes (ABS)

Your first car might not have anti-lock brakes. You still need to know what they can do and how they work.

When driving in difficult conditions
I N C R E A S E   T H E   G A P

Sample questions – Safety margins

SAMPLE QUESTION 11

What is your stopping distance at 70mph?

Mark one answer

☐ **A** 53 metres (175 feet)

☐ **B** 60 metres (197 feet)

☐ **C** 73 metres (240 feet)

☐ **D** 96 metres (315 feet)

Working out the answer to question 11

You are being asked for the stopping distance for **70mph** – this is the top speed for driving on motorways and dual carriageways unless signs show otherwise.

**Remember that: the stopping distance =
the thinking distance + the braking distance**

So that gives you a clue that it will be **a long stopping distance**. Once you've learned the table on page 43, you will get **the right answer – answer D.**

If you find it hard to imagine what the stopping distance at 70mph looks like, here are some tips:

- **The stopping distance at 70mph is 96 metres or 315 feet.**

- **96 metres is about the same length as 24 cars parked bumper to bumper.**

- **24 car lengths is about the size of a football pitch.**

On a motorway, you can see this distance by looking at the blue marker posts beside the road. They are 100 metres apart – that's almost the same as the 96 metres stopping distance at 70mph.

SAMPLE QUESTION 12

If the weather is very hot, the road surface might get soft. Which of the following would be most affected?

Mark one answer

☐ **A** The suspension

☐ **B** Your insurance premium

☐ **C** The braking

☐ **D** The exhaust

Working out the answer to question 12

If you look at the four answers, you'll see that **A** and **D** relate to the **mechanical processes of the vehicle**, and **C** relates **to how you control the vehicle**. This gives you a clue, as any change in the condition of the road surface is most likely to affect your control of the steering and braking. **B is obviously wrong.**

Your control depends on how well your tyres can grip the road. A dry surface gives more grip than a wet surface, and a firm surface gives more grip than a soft surface.

So C is the right answer.

Questions that look alike

Look up the questions about anti-lock brakes in your book of theory test questions. Lots of questions **look the same.** Some are easy and some are hard.

The questions test two things:
- your knowledge of the rules of the road

- your understanding of words to do with driving.

The aim of this book is to help you deal with any words that cause problems for you, so that you can feel confident when you take your theory test.

Check that you know what difficult words mean by looking at the **Glossary** section at the back of this book. It explains what terms like defensive driving and high-sided vehicle mean, as well as words such as priority and tailgating.

SAMPLE QUESTION 13

In normal driving conditions on a fast road in good weather, the distance for safety between you and the vehicle in front should be

Mark one answer

- ☐ **A** one car length
- ☐ **B** two car lengths
- ☐ **C** 2 metres (6 feet 6 inches)
- ☐ **D** a two-second time gap

Working out the answer to question 13

You'll most likely have spotted straight away that this question is about our old friend the **two-second rule** (see page 40). To check that the others are wrong, remember the table of stopping distances (see page 43).

The stopping distance at 70mph is equal to 24 car lengths, so **answers A** and **B** can't be right. As for **answer C**, you know that 2 metres or 6 feet 6 inches is only slightly more than the height of a tall person, so you can cross off that one too.

When you are driving it is easier to judge distances in **time** rather than in feet or metres. Remember that the **faster** you are going the **more time** (distance) you will need to stop.

So D is the right answer.

5. HAZARD AWARENESS

Q. What is the difference between hazard awareness and hazard perception?

- Hazard perception is the name for the part of the theory test that uses video clips. This test is about spotting developing hazards. One of the key skills of good driving, this is called **anticipation.**

- Anticipating hazards means **looking out for them in advance and taking action now.**

- Hazard awareness is about being **alert** whenever you are driving.

That is why some of the questions in this hazard awareness section deal with things that might make you **less alert** – for example:

- feeling tired

- feeling ill

- taking medicines prescribed by your doctor

- drinking alcohol.

Other questions in this section cover:

- noticing road and traffic signs and road markings

- what to do at traffic lights

- when to slow down for hazards ahead.

Taking action to avoid accidents

New drivers have a greater than average chance of being involved in accidents.

Q. Why are new drivers more at risk?

- Lack of experience plays a huge part in why newly qualified drivers are more at risk of being involved in accidents. Research suggests that it takes at least 1,000 miles of driving before a new driver has experienced enough different situations to be able to recognise hazards and react accordingly.

- Research has also shown that new drivers have poorer visual awareness than a more experienced driver – for example they look more at the vehicle in front of them, rather than scanning the area for hazards. This is not intentional but a direct result of inexperience.

- Newly qualified drivers are more likely to be distracted by other tasks within the car, such as using a mobile phone, or by other passengers. Using a hand-held phone is illegal and even a hands-free option takes your attention from the road.

The hazard perception test aims to **'fill the gap' in hazard awareness** for new drivers by making sure they have some proper training to make up for their lack of experience. This should make them safer drivers when they start out on the road alone.

Drivers under 25 make up a small percentage of all drivers on the road but are involved in a high proportion of crashes where someone is seriously hurt or injured.

Looking for clues to developing hazards

As you get more driving experience you will start to learn about the times and places where you are most likely to meet hazards.

Think about some examples.

Rush hour

You know that people take more risks when driving in the rush hour. Maybe they have to drop their children off at school before going to work. Maybe they are late for a meeting. So you have to be prepared for bad driving, such as other drivers pulling out in front of you.

Bin day

Drivers in a hurry may get frustrated if they are held up in traffic because of a hazard such as a dustcart. They may accelerate and pull out to overtake even though they cannot see clearly ahead. You should not blindly follow the lead of another driver. Check for yourself that there are no hazards ahead.

School children

Young children are not very good at knowing how far away a car is from them, and may run into the road unexpectedly. Always be on the lookout for hazards near a school entrance.

Parked cars

Imagine you are driving on a quiet one-way street with cars parked down each side. You wouldn't expect to meet any vehicles coming the other way — but what about children playing? They might run out into the road after a football. It would be difficult to see them because of the parked cars, until they were in the road in front of you.

Scanning the road

Learner drivers tend to look straight ahead of their car and may not notice all the hazards that might be building up **on both sides.**

You will spot more hazards when driving if you train yourself to **scan the road.**

- Practice looking **up and ahead** as far as possible.

- Use all your mirrors to look out for hazards.

- Don't forget you have blind spots when driving – work out where they are and find safe ways of checking all round for hazards.

- Ask your driving instructor to help you with these points.

Q. How is learning to scan the road going to help me pass my theory test?

- As we have said before, the idea of the hazard perception element is to encourage you to get some real experience of driving before you take the theory test.

- If you meet real hazards and learn how to anticipate them, you'll learn how to pass the hazard perception part of the test.

- In the video test you may not be able to look **all around you** as you would when driving a car, but the clips will be as realistic as possible in giving you a wide 'view' of the road ahead.

**Don't forget: not all hazards can be anticipated.
There are bound to be some you
haven't expected.
ALWAYS EXPECT THE UNEXPECTED.**

More examples of hazards

So, what kinds of hazards are we talking about? And what should you do about them?

The list below gives some of the hazards you should look out for when driving along a busy street in town.

After each hazard there are some ideas about what you should be looking out for, and what to do next.

- **You see a bus which has stopped in a lay-by ahead.**

There may be some pedestrians hidden by the bus who are trying to cross the road, or the bus may signal to pull out. Be ready to slow down and stop.

Road markings and road signs sometimes highlight likely hazards for you.

- **You see a white triangle painted on the road surface ahead.**

 This is a hazard warning sign. It tells you that there is a 'Give Way' junction just ahead. Slow down and be ready to stop.

- **You see a sign for a roundabout ahead.**

 Anticipate that other drivers may need to change lane, and be ready to leave them enough room.

- **You come to some roadworks where traffic is controlled by temporary traffic lights.**

Watch out for drivers speeding to get through before the lights change.

Hazard awareness

Hazards may be all around you – not just in front.

- **You look in your rear view mirror and see an emergency vehicle with flashing lights.**

An emergency vehicle wants to pass, so get ready to pull over when it's safe.

- **You see a small child standing with an adult near the edge of the pavement.**

Check if the child is safely holding the adult's hand. Be ready to stop suddenly if the child steps into the road.

Not all hazards are on the road.

- **You notice dustbins put out on the pavement.**

The dustcart could be around the next corner, or bin men could be crossing the road. Be ready to slow down.

Remember to listen for hazards, too.

- **You hear a siren.**

Look all around to find out where the emergency vehicle is. You may have to pull over to let it pass.

You will find out more about different types of hazards, such as what to look for when driving in the country, or in bad weather, in 'Vehicle handling', pages 77–82.

Observation

Taking in information, or observation, is one of the three key skills needed in hazard perception:

- **observation**
- **anticipation**
- **planning**

An easy way to remember this is **O A P** for

Observe – **A**nticipate – **P**lan.

Talking to yourself

It's a good idea to 'talk to yourself' when you're learning to drive – and even after you've passed your test. Talk about all the things you see that could be hazards. Your driving instructor might suggest this as a way of making you concentrate and notice hazards ahead.

Even if you don't talk out loud, you can do a 'running commentary' in your head on everything you see around you as you drive.

For example, you might say to yourself

'I am following a cyclist and the traffic lights ahead are red. *When the lights change I shall allow him/her plenty of time and room to move off.*'

or

'The dual carriageway ahead is starting to look very busy. There is a sign showing that the right lane is closing in 800 yards. *I must get ready to drop back, to allow other vehicles to move into the left-hand lane ahead of me.*'

Note: Don't forget your mirrors. This way, you will notice more hazards, and you will learn to make more sense of the information that you are taking in.

Observation questions

Go to your book of theory test questions and study some of the pictures in the 'Hazard awareness' section.

They include **photographs** of scenes such as:

- a cyclist at traffic lights, seen from the viewpoint of a driver in a car behind the cyclist

- what you see as a driver when you are approaching a level crossing

- what you see when coming up to a 'blind bend'

- a view of the road ahead with traffic building up where one lane is closing.

Look out for situations like these when you are out driving with your instructor, and **use the practice to improve your hazard awareness.**

Did you know?

Our eyes can take in 30 to 40 images per second. We have to make sense of these images, and decide what to do next.

People who have been driving for longer have fewer accidents than new drivers. One of the main reasons is **better hazard perception skills.**

As well as photographs, there are **pictures** of **road and traffic signs**.

Look at these examples:

What do these signs mean?

What actions should you take when you see these signs?

- If you are not sure, look them up in *The Highway Code*.

- Think about *why* the square yellow sign with the two children is in the Vehicle Markings section and not with the rest of the road signs.

Learn your road signs

Notice the information in *The Highway Code* at the bottom of the first page of Traffic signs. It explains that **you won't find every road sign shown there.** You can buy a copy of *Know Your Road Signs* from a bookshop to see some of the extra signs that are not in *The Highway Code*.

Note: In Wales, some signs have the Welsh spelling as well as the English; and in Scotland, some signs have Gaelic spelling. You'll also see some 'old-style' road signs around, which are slightly different too.

Sample questions – Hazard awareness

SAMPLE QUESTION 14

While driving, you see a sign that looks like this ahead. What would you expect drivers ahead of you to do?

Mark one answer

☐ **A** Move into the right lane

☐ **B** Speed up to get ahead

☐ **C** Move into the left lanes

☐ **D** Carry on as normal

> **GET IN LANE**
>
> ↑ ↑ ▬
>   I
>
> **800 yards**

Working out the answer to question 14

Answer A suggests traffic might move into the right lane. This can't be correct, because **it's the right lane that's about to close.** So answer A is wrong.

Answer B is correct in one way – drivers often speed up and overtake to get in front of others when one lane is about to close. But you know from your own experience that motorists who do this are showing **no consideration** for other road users. They will force following drivers to slow down, instead of allowing the traffic to keep flowing. So, answer B is wrong.

If drivers in the right lane were to make **no adjustments at all** to their speed or direction, they would soon be in trouble when the lane closed. So **answer D** is wrong.

As the right lane is going to close, drivers must use their mirrors and indicators to **move across into the left lanes in good time,** when it is safe to do so.

So C is the right answer.

SAMPLE QUESTION 15

You see a set of two amber lights on a pole flashing alternately. What hazard should you look out for?

Mark one answer

- ☐ **A** A level crossing with no gate or barrier
- ☐ **B** A swing bridge
- ☐ **C** An ambulance station
- ☐ **D** A school crossing patrol

Working out the answer to question 15

Look up the rules that deal with Level Crossings in *The Highway Code*. Study the diagram that shows a car waiting at crossing gates.

Level crossings, ambulance stations and swing bridges all have **red lights that flash on and off** to warn you when you must stop.

But this question is about flashing **amber** lights. Amber lights warn of a school crossing patrol.

So answer D is right.

Do you know what a **swing bridge** looks like? If there are none near where you live, ask your driving instructor if there are any nearby that you could go and see.

A **fire station** is another place where you will see red flashing warning lights.

SAMPLE QUESTION 16

Which of the following are likely effects of drinking and driving?

Mark one answer

- ☐ **A** Improved concentration
- ☐ **B** Lack of coordination
- ☐ **C** Colour blindness
- ☐ **D** Improved reaction times

Working out the answers to question 16

To answer this question correctly you need to understand what it's asking you. **'Effects'** means results – so it's asking what will happen to your driving skills if you drink alcohol.

Drinking alcohol **will not** improve your concentration – that is, it won't help you concentrate better. So **answer A** is wrong.

Lack of coordination means not being able to control your own movements properly. Drinking can cause this, so **answer B is potentially the right answer.**

Colour blindness is not caused by drinking alcohol, so **C** is wrong.

Your reaction times will get **worse** not better, so **D** is wrong.

So B is the right answer.

6. VULNERABLE ROAD USERS

Q. What does vulnerable road users mean?

A vulnerable road user is somebody who is at risk from other road users.

Vulnerable road users include:

- pedestrians
- children
- elderly people
- people with disabilities
- cyclists
- motorcycle riders
- horse riders
- learner drivers
- new drivers.

You must drive with extra care when you are near vulnerable road users.

This section explains

- why different types of road users are vulnerable (at risk)
- what you as a driver must do to keep them safe
- the hierarchy of road users.

Vehicle safety and vulnerable road users

Today's vehicles are getting safer all the time for the driver inside the car – but not for those outside. Many road users who are not driving cars have nothing to protect them if they are in an accident with a motor vehicle.

Hierarchy of road users

The idea of the hierarchy of road users is to give those road users most at risk in the event of a collision priority. The road users most likely to be injured in the event of a collision are pedestrians, cyclists, horse riders and motorcyclists, with children, older adults and disabled people being more at risk. But this doesn't mean that these groups can behave how they like; all adults should behave responsibly.

- You should discuss this with your driving instructor so you understand the concept and what you need to do.

- Be sure to read the relevant section in *The Highway Code*.

Cyclists and motorcycle riders

Cyclists and motorcycle riders are more at risk than car drivers because:

- they are more affected by strong winds, or by turbulence (movement of air) caused by other vehicles

- they are more affected by an uneven road surface, and they may have to move out suddenly to avoid a pot-hole

- car drivers often cannot see them.

Always give cyclists plenty of room – especially when they are **coming up to a roundabout.**

Unlike car drivers, cyclists can stay in the left lane on a roundabout while signalling right as they pass an exit, to indicate that they are carrying on round (see the rules for cyclists in *The Highway Code*).

Turn to the section headed Vulnerable road users in your book of theory test questions to see some pictures of this.

You must also give way to cyclists:

- at **toucan crossings**

- in **cycle lanes**.

Pedestrians

Pedestrians most at risk include **elderly people** and **children**.

Elderly people and others who cannot move easily may be slower to cross roads – you must give them plenty of time.

Children don't have a sense of danger on the road; they *can't tell how close a car is, or how fast it is going*. They may run out into the road without looking. Or they may step out behind you when you are reversing – you may not see them because they are small.

When to give way to pedestrians

At any pedestrian crossing, if a pedestrian has started to cross, wait until they have reached the other side. Do not harass them by revving your engine or edging forward.

- **On a light-controlled pedestrian crossing**

At a crossing with lights (pelican, toucan, puffin or equestrian crossings), pedestrians have priority once they have started to cross even if, when on a pelican crossing, the amber lights start flashing.

- **On a zebra crossing**

Once a pedestrian has stepped on to the crossing you **must** stop and wait for them to cross.

Note: You should stop at a zebra crossing if a pedestrian is **waiting** to cross. When you take your practical driving test, you must stop for any pedestrians who are waiting on the pavement at a zebra crossing – even if they haven't stepped onto the crossing yet. However, you must not wave to them to cross.

- **When they have started to cross a road that you want to turn into**

If you want to turn left into a side road and people are crossing the side road on foot, **wait** for them to finish crossing.

People on foot have **priority over car drivers** as part of the hierarchy of road users.

Other types of vulnerable road users

Be prepared to slow down for **animals, learner drivers**, and other more unusual hazards such as people **walking along the road in organised groups** (for example, on a demonstration, or a sponsored walk). There are rules in *The Highway Code* that walkers must follow. But even if they break the rules, make sure you keep to them.

Animals

Drive slowly past horses or other animals. Allow them plenty of space on the road.

Don't frighten them by sounding your horn or revving your engine.

If you see a flock of sheep or a herd of cattle blocking the road, you must:

- stop
- switch off your engine
- and wait until they have left the road.

Did you know?

If a car hits a pedestrian at **40mph**, the pedestrian will **probably be killed**.

Even at **35mph, 50%** of pedestrians hit by cars **will be killed**.

At **20mph**, pedestrians have a better chance of surviving.

This is why you will find 20mph limits and other things to slow traffic in some residential streets and near school entrances.

Sample questions – Vulnerable road users

SAMPLE QUESTION 17

You are approaching a zebra crossing and see a person in a wheelchair waiting to cross. You should

Mark one answer

☐   **A**   carry on driving

☐   **B**   wave them across

☐   **C**   signal to them to wait

☐   **D**   prepare to stop

Working out the answer to question 17

When you see a person waiting to cross at a zebra crossing **you should stop for them**. It does not matter whether they are on foot or in a wheelchair, you should still stop. **So answer A is wrong**.

You should not wave anyone across at a pedestrian crossing; you might put the pedestrian in danger. For example, another car could overtake yours illegally and run into the pedestrian. **So answer B is wrong**.

You should not make any signal to the pedestrian – do not signal to them to wait, because **they have priority** on the crossing. **So answer C is wrong**.

So D is the right answer.

SAMPLE QUESTION 18

You are about to turn left into a side road. You see that pedestrians have started to cross the side road. You should

Mark one answer

☐ **A** keep moving but give them plenty of room

☐ **B** stop and wave them across

☐ **C** give way to the pedestrians

☐ **D** sound your horn and proceed

Working out the answer to question 18

If you keep moving you risk running into the pedestrians; they may stop suddenly, or change direction. **So answer A is wrong**.

Answer B is also wrong – you should not wave them across, but leave the pedestrians **to take care of their own safety**.

If you sound your horn you are harassing the pedestrians, **so answer D is wrong**.

Pedestrians crossing a side road **have priority**, so you should **give way** to them.

So C is the right answer.

7. OTHER TYPES OF VEHICLE

We have already come across some of the other types of vehicles that share the road with you and your car. These include motorbikes and bicycles.

The questions in this part of the theory test are mostly about motorbike riders and cyclists. However, you also need to know what to do about other vehicles, such as:

- buses
- caravans
- trams
- tractors and other farm vehicles
- special vehicles for disabled drivers (powered invalid carriages)
- slow vehicles such as road gritters
- motorway repair vehicles.

Important points to remember about these vehicles:

- many of them can only **move very slowly**
- they **cannot easily stop or change direction.**
- the driver's field of vision may be **restricted** – in other words, the driver cannot see clearly in all directions. This means that car drivers have to **change their driving** to allow them plenty of room.

Cyclists

- Give cyclists plenty of room
- Remember to **keep well back** from cyclists when you are coming up to a junction or a **roundabout** because you cannot be sure what they are going to do.
- On the roundabout they may go in **any direction** – left, right or straight ahead.
- They are allowed to **stay in the left lane** and signal right if they are going to continue round.
- Leave them enough room to **cross in front of you** if they need to.

Cyclists and strong winds

Remember, two-wheeled vehicles are easily blown off-course by strong crosswinds. So allow plenty of space when you overtake a cyclist, in case they swerve suddenly.

Look out for cyclists

- It can be **hard to see** cyclists in busy **town traffic**.
- It can also be hard to see them coming when you are waiting to turn out at a **junction**. They can be hidden by other vehicles (see below).

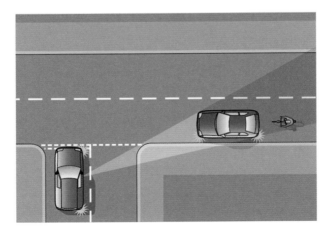

Always be on the lookout for cyclists. You should **check your mirror** to make sure you do not trap a cyclist on your left when you are turning left into a side road.

- Check your **blind spots** for cyclists, too.

Controlling your vehicle near cyclists

When you are following a cyclist, you must be able to drive **as slowly as they do**, and keep your vehicle under control. Only overtake when you can allow them plenty of room, and it is safe to do so.

Cycle lanes

- Cycle lanes are for cyclists. Car drivers should not use them.

- A cycle lane is marked by a **white line** on the road.

- A **solid white line** means **you must not drive or park in the cycle lane** during the hours it is in use.

- A **broken white line** means you should drive or park in it **only if there is no alternative**. You should not park there at any time when there are **waiting restrictions**.

Motorcycles

- Motorcycles are easily blown off course by strong winds.

- If you see a motorcyclist overtaking a **high-sided vehicle** such as a lorry, keep well back. The lorry may shield the motorcyclist from the wind as it is overtaking, but then a sudden gust could blow the motorcyclist off-course.

- It can be **hard to see** a motorcyclist when you are waiting at a **junction**. Always look out for them.

- If you see a motorcyclist **looking over their shoulder**, it could mean that they will **soon give a signal to turn right**. This applies to cyclists too. Keep back to give them plenty of room.

- Motorcyclists and cyclists sometimes have to **swerve to avoid hazards** such as bumps in the road, patches of ice and drain covers. As before – give them plenty of room.

When you overtake a cyclist, a motorcyclist or a horse rider, **give them at least as much room as you would a car.**

Long vehicles

- Like cyclists, long vehicles coming up to roundabouts may **stay in the left lane even if they intend to turn right**.

This is because they need lots of **room to manoeuvre (turn).**

Keep well back so they have room to turn.

- Take great **care when overtaking** long or high-sided vehicles.

Before you pull out to overtake, make sure you have **a clear view of the road ahead**.

Buses and trams

- Always **give way to buses** when they signal to pull out.

- Always **give way to trams**; they cannot steer to avoid you.

- Don't try to **overtake** a tram.

Trams are **quiet** vehicles – you cannot rely on engine noise to warn you that a tram is coming.

Take extra care when you see this sign, because **trams are sometimes allowed to go when car drivers are not**.

Tractors and slow-moving vehicles

- Always **be patient** if you are following a slow vehicle.

Drivers of slow vehicles will usually try to find a safe place to pull in to let the traffic go past. Keep well back, so that you can see the road ahead. Allow a safe distance in case they slow down or stop.

Slow vehicles are not allowed on motorways because they cannot keep up with the fast-moving traffic. Vehicles not allowed on motorways include:

- motorcycles under 50cc
- bicycles
- tractors and other farm vehicles
- powered invalid carriages.

For more on motorway rules, see pages 83–90 of this book.

Sample questions – Other types of vehicle

SAMPLE QUESTION 19

You are following a motorcyclist who is travelling slowly. Which of the following signs alerts you to take special care?

Mark one answer

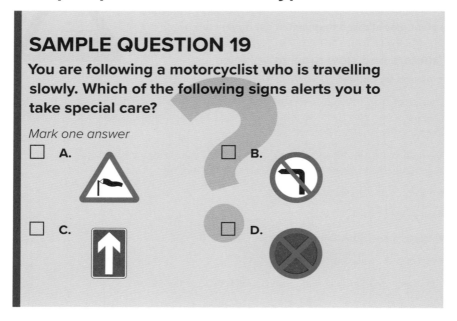

☐ A.

☐ B.

☐ C.

☐ D.

Working out the answer to question 19

Look up these signs in *The Highway Code*. You will see that **Sign A** means 'side winds', **Sign B** means 'no left turn', **Sign C** means 'one-way traffic' and **Sign D** means 'no stopping (clearway)'.

You know that strong side winds can blow a motorcyclist off course. **Sign A** is the sign for high winds.

So A is the right answer.

SAMPLE QUESTION 20

You are following a long vehicle coming up to a crossroads. The driver of the long vehicle signals left, but moves to the right towards the middle of the road. What should you do?

Mark one answer

- ☐ **A** Accelerate to pass the long vehicle before it starts to turn
- ☐ **B** Wait until it starts to slow down before you overtake
- ☐ **C** Stay well back to give the long vehicle plenty of room
- ☐ **D** Assume the signal is wrong – it is actually going to turn right

Working out the answer to question 20

Answers A, B and **D** are all **very dangerous** actions. If you try to overtake you will endanger yourself and other road users.

A long vehicle needs plenty of room to go round a corner, so may need to pull out into the centre of the road before making the turn.

So C is the right answer.

SAMPLE QUESTION 21

You see a bus ahead signalling to move off. You should

Mark one answer

- ☐ **A** carry on at the same speed
- ☐ **B** use your horn
- ☐ **C** accelerate past the bus before it moves out
- ☐ **D** look out for pedestrians appearing suddenly

Working out the answers to question 21

You should **always give way to a bus** which is signalling to pull out. So **answer A** and **answer C** are both wrong.

Sounding your horn is not helpful, so **answer B** is also wrong.

When you follow a bus you should **keep a look-out for pedestrians** crossing in front of or behind the bus.

So D is the right answer.

SAMPLE QUESTION 22

You are driving on a road where there are tram lines. Why should you take extra care?

Mark one answer

- [ ] **A** Trams do not stop for cars
- [ ] **B** Trams have no lights
- [ ] **C** Trams cannot steer to avoid you
- [ ] **D** Trams do not have a horn

Working out the answers to question 22

Answer A is not true, although sometimes trams may have priority over cars. **Answer B** is obviously wrong, as trams need to have lights like any other vehicle on the road. Likewise, they also have horns so **answer D** is wrong too.

Trams have to run on tram lines, so they **cannot steer to avoid you**.

So C is the right answer.

8. VEHICLE HANDLING

The questions in this section test how much you know about controlling your vehicle.

Your control is affected by:

- the **road surface** – is it rough or smooth? Are there any holes or bumps? Are there any traffic-calming measures such as humps or chicanes?

- the **weather conditions** – you have to drive in different ways when there is fog, snow, ice or heavy rain.

Other questions cover:

- **driving on country roads** – on narrow and one-way roads, humpback bridges, steep hills and fords.

- There are also questions that need **technical knowledge** – for example, on engine braking, brake fade and coasting your vehicle.

- This section also has some questions on **overtaking** and **parking**.

Road surface

- The **condition** of the road surface can affect the way your vehicle handles (drives on the road).

Your vehicle handles better on a smooth surface than on a surface that is damaged, bumpy or full of holes. If you have to drive on an uneven surface, **keep your speed down** so that you have full control of your vehicle, even if your steering wheel is jolted.

Take care also where there are **tramlines** on the road.

- The **layout** of the road affects the way your vehicle handles.

You may have to adjust your driving for traffic calming measures such as **traffic humps** (sometimes called 'sleeping policemen') and **chicanes**. These are double bends that have been put into the road layout to slow the traffic down. The sign before the chicane tells you **who has priority**.

Traffic calming measures are often used in residential areas or near school entrances **to make it safer for pedestrians**.

Weather conditions

Bad weather (adverse weather) such as **heavy rain, ice** or **snow** affects the way your vehicle handles. **If you drive too fas**t in adverse weather, your tyres may lose their grip on the road when you try to brake. This means the car may skid or aquaplane.

- Aquaplaning means sliding out of control on a wet surface.

Remember the two-second rule?

You should **double** the two-second gap to **four seconds** when driving in rain, and increase the gap by as much as **ten times** when there is **ice** on the road.

Q. *What are the rules for driving in snow?*

- In snow, the best advice is **do not drive at all** unless you really have to make a journey. If you have to drive in snowy conditions, leave extra time for your journey and keep to the main roads.

- You can fit **snow chains** to your tyres to increase their grip in deep snow.

Q. *What about driving in fog?*

- In fog your *field of vision* can be down to a few metres. Your vehicle is fitted with **fog lights** to help you see and be seen in fog. But you must know *how and when to use them*.

Look up the three rules about fog lights in *The Highway Code*. You'll see that the key points to remember are:

- **don't dazzle** other road users with your fog lights

- **switch them off** as soon as you can see better (once visibility improves).

Country driving

If you have had most of your driving lessons in a town, you need to know how to drive on **narrow country roads**. Some are only wide enough for one vehicle ('single-track'), and some are on very steep hills.

Your control of the **gears, clutch and brakes** will be important if you have to follow a tractor very slowly **up a hill.** On a **steep downward slope** you have to make sure your vehicle does not 'run away'.

Vehicle handling

On country roads you might find **humpback bridges** and **fords**. The signs below warn you of these hazards.

- Find out what you must do **first** after you have driven through a ford.

Technical knowledge

We have already mentioned **engine braking.** Understanding how engine braking works is part of good vehicle handling.

Note: If you press the footbrake constantly on a long hill, you may get brake fade. If you're not sure, check what that means in the **Glossary** at the back of this book.

Use the gears to control your vehicle on a downhill slope (or 'gradient'). If you put the vehicle in neutral, or drive with the clutch down, and **coast** down the hill your vehicle will increase speed beyond what is safe.

- Coasting is wrong and dangerous.
- Some people believe coasting saves fuel, this is incorrect.

Look back to page 37 for another example of a question where you have to use your technical knowledge. Question 12 on page 48 was about the fact that **hot weather can affect the way your vehicle handles**, because the road surface can become soft.

Remember that if there is **sudden heavy rain** after a dry hot spell, the road surface can get very **slippery**.

Sample questions – Vehicle handling

SAMPLE QUESTION 23

When travelling in conditions of heavy rain, your separation distance should be

Mark one answer

- ☐ **A** halved
- ☐ **B** multiplied by two
- ☐ **C** up to ten times greater
- ☐ **D** the same as in normal conditions

Working out the answer to question 23

If you have learned the **two-second rule**, you should have no problem with this question. Your separation distance should be doubled or 'multiplied by two'.

Answer A must be wrong because 'halved' means 'divided by two'. **Answer C** would be right if the question was about driving in icy conditions, when you have to multiply your safety margin by ten. The question asks about driving in 'heavy rain', so **answer D** is unlikely to be right.

So B is the right answer.

SAMPLE QUESTION 24

What do traffic calming measures do?

Mark one answer

- ☐ **A** They tell drivers when to overtake
- ☐ **B** They reduce road rage
- ☐ **C** They slow down the traffic
- ☐ **D** They decrease pedestrian safety

Working out the answer to question 24

Traffic calming measures include speed humps, chicanes and rumble strips.

They are there to make traffic slow down.

You should not overtake where there are traffic calming measures, so **answer A** is wrong. **Answer B** is wrong too: road rage means angry drivers, and this question is about **calming** traffic. Traffic calming measures **increase** pedestrian safety so **answer D** is wrong.

So C is the right answer.

SAMPLE QUESTION 25

What rule applies to the use of fog lights?

Mark one answer

- [ ] **A** Use them only in heavy traffic
- [ ] **B** Never use them on motorways
- [ ] **C** Only use them with dipped headlights
- [ ] **D** Remember to turn them off once visibility improves

Working out the answer to question 25

Answer A does not make sense – you might be driving on a lonely country road in fog and need to switch on fog lights. So answer **A** is wrong.

You may need to use fog lights on a motorway in very heavy fog, so **answer B** is wrong. But you should always switch them off as soon as the fog starts to clear, so that you **do not dazzle other drivers**.

There is no rule in *The Highway Code* about using fog lights with dipped headlights. You have to decide what will best help you see and be seen – dipped or full beam headlights. So **answer C** is wrong.

So D is the right answer.

9. MOTORWAY RULES

Q. Under what circumstances are learner drivers allowed on the motorway?

- Learner drivers are allowed on motorways as long as they are in a car with dual controls and under the supervision of an ADI. It will be up to your driving instructor if you use a motorway during your driving lesson.

Whether you use a motorway as a learner driver or not, as soon as you pass your driving test you will be legally allowed to drive on motorways. You need to know all the **rules in advance**, so that you are confident and ready to cope with motorway driving when you pass your test. You'll need skills including:

- using **lanes** properly,

- knowing when it is safe to **overtake**

- **controlling your vehicle** at speed.

There are some **major roads and dual carriageways** that learners can drive on which are very much like motorways. You may drive on some of these during your driving test, so that your examiner can see how well you cope with hazards at **higher speeds**.

If you are learning to drive with a good driving school, you will also have the chance to book a **motorway lesson with your instructor** after you have passed your test. It makes sense to take up this offer before you drive on a motorway alone for the first time.

Q. What are the differences between motorways and other roads?

- On a motorway, traffic is **moving at high speed all the time.**

- **All lanes** are in use.

- **No stopping** is allowed on a motorway – traffic only slows or comes to a stop because of accidents or other types of hold-up.

- You always **leave a motorway on the left**, via a slip road.

- To the left of the inside lane (left-hand lane) on a motorway is an extra lane called the **hard shoulder**. You can only drive on this **in an emergency**.

- Special **signs and signals** are used on motorways. These include signs above the road on overhead gantries, signs on the central reservation, and amber and red flashing lights.

Some **road users are not allowed on motorways**. These include:

- pedestrians, cyclists and powered mobility scooters

- horses and other animals

- motorcycles under 50cc

- slow-moving vehicles, tractors and farm vehicles and invalid carriages

- learner drivers unaccompanied by an ADI.

Checks before your journey

Be extra careful about doing all your **regular checks** before you set out on a motorway journey; you cannot stop on the motorway to fix small problems, and no one wants to break down in the middle of fast traffic.

Always check:

- the oil and coolant levels

- the screen wash container

- tyres and tyre pressures

- fuel gauge

- that all mirrors and windows are free of dirt, grease, snow or ice

- that the horn works.

Many of these checks are **legally necessary**, as well as important for your safety.

How to move on to the motorway

- Join the motorway by **building up your speed on the slip road** to match the speed of traffic in the left lane of the motorway.

- Use **MSM (Mirrors – Signal – Manoeuvre)** and move into the flow of traffic when it is safe to do so.

Changing lanes and overtaking

Driving on a motorway needs all the skills you have learned about **anticipation and forward planning.**

You should:

- make good use of all mirrors, and check your blind spots

- signal to move out in plenty of time

- look out for hazards ahead in the lane you want to move to

- not go ahead if it will force another vehicle to brake or swerve

- keep a safe distance from the vehicle in front.

Always ask yourself these three questions before overtaking – especially on motorways:
1. Is it safe?
2. Is it legal?
3. Is it necessary?

Motorway rules

Take a break

When you drive on motorways you will sometimes see signs that say 'Tiredness can kill – take a break.'

This is very good advice. Motorways can be boring to drive, with long stretches of road that look the same for miles. A major cause of accidents is **drivers falling asleep at the wheel**. Plan your journey so that you have time to get out, stretch your legs and have a drink or snack.

The rules you need to know

- **Keep to the left-hand lane unless you are overtaking** and move back to the left lane as soon as it is safe to do so.

Sometimes you need to stay in the centre lane for a time – for example, when a line of lorries is travelling up a hill in the left lane.

Stay in the centre lane until you have passed the hazard, then signal left and return to the left lane.

- **Never reverse, park, walk** or **drive in the wrong direction** on the motorway.

- Don't **exceed the speed limit.**

This is normally 70mph, but lower speed limits may be signed when the road is busy, or in bad weather.

- Keep to the **correct separation distance** (see pages 42 and 43).

- Don't **overtake on the left.**

If traffic is moving slowly in all three lanes you may find that the lane on the left is moving faster than the one to its right for a short time. Or the left lane may be signed for traffic turning off at the next junction only. But these are exceptions to the rule.

- If luggage falls from your vehicle, **do not get out to pick it up.** Stop at the next emergency phone and tell the police what has happened.

Posts on the edge of the motorway show the way to the nearest emergency phone. You should use these phones rather than your mobile, because the **emergency phone** connects directly to the Highways Agency and tells them exactly where you are on the motorway.

- **Don't stop on the hard shoulder except in an emergency.**

The hard shoulder is an extremely dangerous place, more than 30% of accidents on the hard shoulder are fatal or serious.

Rules for using the hard shoulder

- Stop as far to the left as possible with your wheels turned to the left and, if you can, near an emergency phone.

- Switch on your hazard warning lights.

- Use the left-hand door to get out of the vehicle, and make sure your passengers do too.

- Get everyone away from the road – if possible, behind the barrier or up the bank.

- Leave animals in the vehicle unless they aren't safe there.

- Phone the Highways Agency with full details of where you are, then go back and wait in a safe place near your vehicle.

Smart motorways

Some UK motorways are now 'smart' motorways, which use technology to manage the flow of traffic. This includes temporarily or permanently opening the hard shoulder to traffic, and using electronic signs to close lanes or reduce speed limits as needed. If you are going to drive on a smart motorway you should familiarise yourself with the advice given by Highways England on gov.uk/guidance/how-to-drive-on-a-smart-motorway.

Motorway signs

Here are some of the traffic signs you will find on the motorway. These signs are lit up when they are needed to warn you:

- that there is an **accident** or a **traffic jam ahead**

- that a **lane is going to close**

- that a **lower speed limit** is in force

- that you will have **to cross to the other carriageway** because of roadworks (this is called a '**contraflow**')

- that there is **bad weather** ahead.

Sample questions – Motorway rules

SAMPLE QUESTION 26

The correct way to join a motorway is to

Mark one answer

- ☐ **A** drive on the hard shoulder until you see a gap
- ☐ **B** come to a stop on the end of the slip road
- ☐ **C** speed up to overtake the traffic on your right
- ☐ **D** give way to traffic already on the motorway

Working out the answer to question 26

This question is about three of the rules we have covered in this chapter.

Look back to page 87; the hard shoulder is **only for use in an emergency,** so **answer A** is wrong.

When joining a motorway you should **build up speed on the slip road** to match that of the traffic in the left lane of the motorway – you **should not come to a stop** before you join the motorway, as you might on non-motorway roads. So **answer B** is wrong.

Look back to page 86. Speeding up to overtake traffic on your right means the same as **overtaking on the left,** which is not allowed. So **answer C** is wrong.

Although you should build up your speed to match the traffic already on the motorway, you should not accelerate to race past it – if necessary, you must slow down and **give way** to traffic already on the motorway.

So D is the right answer.

SAMPLE QUESTION 27

Which vehicles are prohibited from using the motorway?

Mark one answer

- ☐ **A** Powered mobility scooters
- ☐ **B** Motorcycles over 50 cc
- ☐ **C** Double-deck buses
- ☐ **D** Cars with automatic transmission

Working out the answers to question 27

If you have learned the information given on page 84 you will be able to answer this question.

The only 'catch' is in **answer B** – 'above 50cc'. You'll remember that motorcycles below 50cc are not allowed on the motorway; but those **above** 50cc are allowed.

So A is the right answer.

SAMPLE QUESTION 28

When are you allowed to stop on a motorway?

Mark one answer

☐ **A** If you need to check your map

☐ **B** Because you are tired and need a break

☐ **C** When told to stop by the police

☐ **D** To answer your mobile phone

Working out the answers to question 28

This is a slightly tricky question because the first answer that comes to mind would be 'Never!' – you cannot stop on a motorway.

When you think about it, you know that sometimes you **do** have to stop, for example, if you break down – however this is not one of the options.

You must always stop if a person in authority such as a police officer tells you to, or if you see red lights on the signs above the road.

So C is the right answer.

10. RULES OF THE ROAD

'Rules of the road' is a good way to describe what is in *The Highway Code.*

The questions that come under this heading in the theory test book include several on road signs and road markings. There are lots more road sign questions in the section on Road and traffic signs.

Several of the topics listed in this section have already come up. Other questions in this section cover:

- speed limits
- overtaking
- parking
- lanes and roundabouts
- clearways
- box junctions
- crossroads
- pedestrian crossings
- towing caravans and trailers.

Speed limits

Driving too fast for the road, traffic or weather conditions **causes accidents**.

The right speed for the road

Make sure that you **keep below the speed limit** shown on the signs for the road you are on.

30mph in a
built-up area

50mph on a long,
twisty country road

or as low as 20mph in
a residential area with
speed humps or traffic-
calming measures

> **The national speed limit for cars on a dual carriageway is 70mph. This is also the maximum speed for motorway driving.**

National speed limit

When you leave a built-up area you will usually see this sign.

Q. Does this mean I can drive as fast as I like?

- This sign tells you that the national speed limit for this type of road applies here.
- The national speed limit for cars on a normal road (single carriageway outside a built-up area) is 60mph.
- So on this road you must drive below 60mph even if it is straight and empty.

The right speed for the conditions

If it is raining or there is snow and ice on the road or if you are driving in a high wind you will have to drive **more slowly than the maximum speed limit.** This will keep you and other road users safe.

- Remember – you have to **double** the time you allow for stopping and braking in wet weather. Allow **even more time** in snow and ice.

- You need to be extra careful when driving in **fog**.

The right speed for your vehicle

Some other vehicles have lower speed limits than cars.

Study this table, and check the section on speed limits in *The Highway Code*.

TYPE OF VEHICLE	Built-up areas*	Elsewhere		Motorways
		Single carriageways	Dual carriageways	
	MPH	MPH	MPH	MPH
Cars & motorcycles (including car derived vans up to 2 tonnes maximum laden weight)	30	60	70	70
Cars towing caravans or trailers (including car derived vans and motorcycles)	30	50	60	60
Buses & coaches (not exceeding 12 metres in overall length)	30	50	60	70
Goods vehicles (not exceeding 7.5 tonnes maximum laden weight)	30	50	60	70†
Goods vehicles (exceeding 7.5 tonnes maximum laden weight)	30	50‡	60§	60

* The 30mph limit usually applies to all traffic on all roads with street lighting unless signs show otherwise.
† 60mph if articulated or towing a trailer.
‡ 40mph in Scotland.
§ 50mph in Scotland.

Parking rules

There are some general rules about parking that all drivers should know.

- Whenever you can, you should use off-street car parks or parking bays. These are marked out with white lines on the road.

- Never park where your vehicle could be a danger to other road users.

Where not to park

- On the pavement

- At a bus stop

- In front of someone's drive

- Opposite a traffic island

- Near a school entrance

- On a pedestrian crossing (or inside the zigzag lines either side of the crossing)

- Near a junction

- On a clearway

- On a motorway.

Special rules

Look for signs that tell you

- that you cannot park there at certain times of the day
- that only certain people can park in that place.

Examples of these include:

- bus lanes
- cycle lanes
- residents' parking zones
- roads edged with red or yellow lines.

Blue badges are given to people with disabilities. Do not park in a space reserved for a disabled driver – **even if that is the only place left to park**. A disabled driver may need to park there. You will break the law if you park in that space.

Parking at night

- If you park at night on a road that has a speed limit higher than 30mph, you must **switch on your parking lights**, even if you have parked in a lay-by.
- When parking at night, always park facing in **the same direction as the traffic flow**.
- If your vehicle has a **trailer**, you must switch on parking lights, even if the road has a 30mph speed limit.

Sample questions – Rules of the road

SAMPLE QUESTION 29

You decide to park your car overnight on a road that has a speed limit of 40mph. You should

Mark one answer

- [ ] **A** position your vehicle to face the oncoming traffic
- [ ] **B** put your parking lights on before you leave the vehicle
- [ ] **C** put dipped headlights on before you leave the vehicle
- [ ] **D** park under a street light

Working out the answer to question 29

When you leave your vehicle in a street overnight, you should park facing **in the same direction as the traffic flow** – not facing the oncoming traffic. So **answer A** is the wrong answer.

Answer D is partly right. It is always a good idea to choose a well lit parking place, to stop crime. So **answer D** could be the right answer – unless any of the others is *definitely* right.

To check **answers B** and **C**, look back to page 95. If you park overnight in a road **with a speed limit higher than 30mph** you must **switch on parking lights**. This question is about a road with a **40mph** speed limit.

So B is the right answer.

Parking lights are also known as **side lights** or **position lights**.

SAMPLE QUESTION 30

You are driving along a street in a town but there are no speed limit signs. How can you tell whether you are in a 30mph area?

Mark one answer

- [ ] **A** By the double yellow lines on the road
- [ ] **B** By the pedestrian islands in the middle of the road
- [ ] **C** By the hazard warning lines on the road
- [ ] **D** By the street lighting

Working out the answer to question 30

Hazard warning lines do not tell you about speed limits. They tell you to take extra care when overtaking or at junctions. So **answer C** is wrong.

Double yellow lines (meaning no waiting) or pedestrian islands are often found in busy streets, where you must watch out for pedestrians and other hazards. So **answers A** and **B** might be right.

However, *The Highway Code* says that the speed limit where there are **street lights** is normally 30mph.

So D is the right answer.

SAMPLE QUESTION 31

You must not stop on a clearway

Mark one answer

- [ ] **A** at any time
- [ ] **B** during the daytime
- [ ] **C** between 4pm and 6pm
- [ ] **D** during the night

Working out the answer to question 31

You can answer this question very easily if you know the road and traffic signs in *The Highway Code*.

The rule for a clearway is simple: no stopping **at any time**.

So A is the right answer.

SAMPLE QUESTION 32

You are driving a car towing a trailer on a single carriageway road and you see the sign for National Speed Limit. What is your highest allowed speed?

Mark one answer

☐ **A** 40mph
☐ **B** 50mph
☐ **C** 60mph
☐ **D** 70mph

Working out the answer to question 32

When you have passed your driving test you will be allowed to tow a small trailer. So you need to know the rules.

Look back to the speed limit table on page 93. You will see that the national speed limit for cars is 70mph on a dual carriageway and **60mph on a single carriageway**. Both go down by **10mph** when the car is towing a trailer.

So B is the right answer.

11. ROAD AND TRAFFIC SIGNS

Look up the chapter Road and traffic signs in your book of theory test questions. You will see that it takes up quite a few pages.

- This is because most of the questions have a picture of a road sign or marking, so don't worry about how long the section is.

You will also see that a lot of questions use the same words, but the pictures are different for each question.

- Those words are: 'What does this sign mean?'

So you can see that you need to know The Highway Code very well to answer the questions in this section.

Q. Will I have to learn The Highway Code off by heart?

- You can try to learn as much of it as possible. There are other ways you can help yourself to get to know the road signs. Look at the next page for some tips on how to get started.

Be aware

As you walk or drive around, **look at the road signs** you see in the street, and the different **markings painted on the road surface**.

If you are on foot:

Look at the signs and signals that all road users must obey, whether they are in a car or walking. For example, when you use a pedestrian crossing, check what kind of crossing it is (such as a pelican, toucan or zebra crossing).

Check whether you know the following:

- What are the rules for pedestrians and drivers coming up to the crossing?

- What kinds of crossings are controlled by traffic lights?

- What is different about a zebra crossing?

If you are having a driving lesson:

Look well ahead so that you see all the signs that tell you what to do next, and obey them in good time.

Q. Surely in the test the examiner will tell me what to do next?

- When you take your driving test the examiner will tell you when to move off, when to make a turn and when to carry out one of the set manoeuvres. But they will expect you to watch out for lane markings on the road and signs giving directions, and to decide how to react to these yourself.

- The examiner will ask you to drive without junction-by-junction directions for a short time to assess your independent driving skills. The examiner will continue to assess your driving skills but will not be assessing your ability to remember a route, so you can still ask the examiner to confirm which direction you should be going in. Your driving instructor will help you to practise this skill.

Q. What should I do when I see lots of signs all in the same place at once?

- If you see several signs all on the same post, it can be confusing. The general rule is to **start at the top** and read down the post.

- The sign at the top tells you about the **first hazard** you have to look out for.

If you are a passenger in a car on a **motorway**, look at the motorway signs, because you need to know them, even though you can't drive on a motorway yet yourself.

Check that you can answer the following:

- What colour are the signs at the side of the motorway?
- What do the light signals above the road tell you?
- What signs tell you that you are coming to an exit?

Know your shapes

Road and traffic signs come in **three main shapes**. Get to know them.

You must learn what the signs mean.

Circles

Signs in **circles** tell you **to do** (blue) or **not do** (red) something – they **give orders.**

Triangles

Signs in **triangles** tell you of a **hazard** ahead – they **give warnings.**

Rectangles

Signs in **rectangles** tell you about **where you are** or **where you are going** – they **give information.**

Did you know?

There is only one sign which is **octagonal**. This is the sign for **STOP.** The eight-sided shape makes the sign stand out more.

Sample questions – Road and traffic signs

SAMPLE QUESTION 33

What does this sign mean?

Mark one answer

- [ ] **A** Cars and motorcycles only
- [ ] **B** No overtaking
- [ ] **C** No motor vehicles
- [ ] **D** Clearway

Working out the answer to question 33

This sign shows two vehicles – a car and a motorcycle – in black with a **red circle** round them.

Signs with circles **give orders**; and red tells you **not** to do something (see page 101). So the answer is likely to be one starting with '**No** ...'. So **answer A** is wrong.

The sign for a **clearway** is a red cross on a blue background. So **answer D** must be wrong.

The sign for **No overtaking** shows a red car next to a black car. So **answer B** is wrong.

So C is the right answer.

SAMPLE QUESTION 34

Which sign means 'Turn left ahead'?

Mark one answer

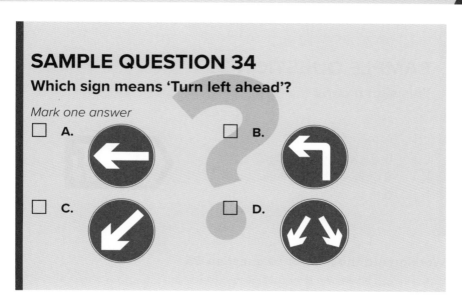

☐ A.

☐ B.

☐ C.

☐ D.

Working out the answer to question 34

All of these signs look similar – they all have white arrows on a blue background.

Make sure you study *The Highway Code* so that you know the difference between similar signs.

There is a clue in the words of the question – 'Turn left ahead'. You must look for the sign which tells you to do something *a little further along the road*.

The arrow in sign **B** goes **up first,** and **then left.**

So B is the right answer.

The other signs mean:

A – Turn left

C – Keep left

D – Pass either side

SAMPLE QUESTION 35

This sign means

Mark one answer

- ☐ **A** Tourist attraction
- ☐ **B** Trams crossing ahead
- ☐ **C** Level crossing ahead
- ☐ **D** Beware of trains

Working out the answer to question 35

You can cross off **answer B** straight away, because the sign shows a train and not a tram.

Answers C and **D** are both about trains, but the sign for a level crossing is a gate, or a train, in a red triangle. So **answers C and D** are wrong.

The shape of this sign tells you it's giving you **information**, instead of a warning or an order. From reading *The Highway Code*, you will know that tourist attraction signs are usually brown.

So A is the right answer.

12. DOCUMENTS

This is quite a short section in your book of theory test questions and is different from the other sections.

This is because it does not deal with driving skills or most knowledge in *The Highway Code*. Instead, it covers all the paperwork you need to know about when you start learning to drive.

In this section there are questions about:

- driving licences

- insurance

- MOT certificate

- Vehicle Excise Duty

- Vehicle Registration Certificate (log book).

This section also covers:

- who can supervise a learner driver

- changes you must tell the licensing authority about.

Driving licence

If you are learning to drive, you need a provisional licence.

- You must have a **valid** licence to drive legally. 'Valid' means correct, up to date and paid for.

- All licences are issued as a photocard, which contains your signature.

- Take good care of your provisional licence. If you lose it by mistake, you can get another one but you will have to pay a fee, and wait for the new licence to come.

- When you pass your test you can apply for a **full licence**.

Insurance

You must always have a valid **insurance certificate** that covers you at least for **third party liability**.

- If you are learning with a good driving school, you are covered by their insurance while you are in the driving school car. When you are in your own or anybody else's car, you must have insurance.

Q. What does 'third party liability' mean?

- Third party insurance cover usually comes as '**Third Party, Fire and Theft**'.

It is a basic insurance policy that will pay for repairs to another person's car and allows you to claim on the other driver's insurance if you are in an accident that was not your fault.

If you have **comprehensive** insurance, the policy will pay for repairs to your vehicle even when the accident was your fault.

MOT certificate

Cars and motorcycles must have their first **MOT test** three years after they are new and first registered. After that, they must have an MOT test every year.

The MOT test checks:

- that your vehicle is **roadworthy** – that is, all the parts work properly and the vehicle is safe to drive

- that it keeps to the legal limits for **exhaust emissions** – that is, the levels of pollution in the gas that comes from the exhaust.

If your vehicle is over three years old you must not drive it without a valid MOT certificate – unless you are on your way to get an MOT and you have booked it in advance.

Vehicle Excise Duty (Road Tax)

Vehicle Excise Duty is the tax that the government charges you to drive your vehicle on the roads, more commonly known as **road tax**. To drive or keep a vehicle on the road you must keep your tax up to date.

Before you can tax your vehicle, you **must show proof** of:

- a valid insurance certificate

- a valid MOT certificate (if the vehicle is over three years' old).

You can tax your vehicle online, by phone or at certain post offices.

If you want to keep a vehicle off the public road you must inform the DVLA by completing a **Statutory Off Road Vehicle Notification (SORN)**. It is an offence not to do so. You then won't have to pay the Vehicle Excise Duty. The SORN is valid until your vehicle is taxed, sold or scrapped.

Vehicle Registration Certificate

The Vehicle Registration Certificate has all the important details about **you and your vehicle**, such as the make and model of the vehicle. It also has your name and address as the **registered keeper** of the vehicle.

This is a record of the vehicle's history and is sometimes called **the log book.**

Changes you must tell the licensing authority about

You **must** tell the Driver and Vehicle Licensing Agency (DVLA):

- when you buy or sell a car

- if you change your name or address.

This is because your details go onto the **Vehicle Registration Certificate.**

Supervising a learner driver

Q. Who is allowed to supervise a learner driver?

As a learner driver, you cannot drive on your own. If you are not with your driving instructor, you must be supervised by a person:

- who is at least **21 years old**

- and has **a full licence** for the kind of car you drive*

- and has had that licence for **at least three years**.

*Note: if a person has a licence to drive an **automatic** car only, they cannot supervise a learner in a **manual** car.

Sample questions – Documents

SAMPLE QUESTION 36

For how long is an MOT certificate normally valid?

Mark one answer

- ☐ **A** 10,000 miles
- ☐ **B** 30,000 miles
- ☐ **C** Three years from the date of issue
- ☐ **D** One year from the date of issue

Working out the answer to question 36

MOT certificates are not about how many miles the car has travelled. **So answers A and B** are wrong.

The mention of 'three years' might remind you that the vehicle needs its first MOT three years after it is registered, but **C** is also the wrong answer.

An MOT certificate is valid for one year. When it gets near to the date on the certificate you must book an appointment for your next MOT test.

So D is the right answer.

SAMPLE QUESTION 37

If someone supervises you while you are learning to drive, how old must they be?

Mark one answer

- ☐ **A** Over 18
- ☐ **B** Over 25
- ☐ **C** 21 or older
- ☐ **D** Any age if they have passed their test

Working out the answer to question 37

Anyone who supervises a learner driver must be at least 21 years old and must have held a full licence for 3 years.

So C is the right answer.

SAMPLE QUESTION 38

What is the minimum insurance cover you MUST have before you drive on the road?

Mark one answer

☐ **A** Third party, fire and theft

☐ **B** Fully comprehensive

☐ **C** Third party only

☐ **D** Excess only

Working out the answer to question 38

Although third party insurance is usually sold as 'Third Party, Fire and Theft', the law says only that you must have 'a valid insurance certificate covering you for third party liability'.

'Liability' means being responsible for something by law; for example, if you have to pay for the repairs to someone else's car if you have a crash.

So C is the right answer.

13. INCIDENTS, ACCIDENTS AND EMERGANCIES

The questions in this section are about helping anyone who is hurt in a road accident.

Some people think they might do more harm than good if they try to help. But if you have some knowledge of first aid you will not panic if you are first on the scene at an accident. You could even save a life. Look up accidents and first aid in *The Highway Code*.

Other questions in this section cover:

- what to do when warning lights come on in your vehicle
- what to do if you break down
- safety equipment to carry with you
- when to use hazard warning lights
- what to do – and what not to do – at the scene of an accident.

Basic first aid

What to do at an accident scene

The Highway Code advises that the following information may be of general assistance, but there's no substitute for proper training. Any first aid given at the scene of an incident should be looked on only as a temporary measure until the emergency services arrive. If you haven't had any first aid training, the following points could be helpful.

1. Deal with danger

Further collisions and fire are the main dangers following a crash. Approach any vehicle involved with care, watching out for spilt oil or broken glass. Switch off all engines and, if possible, warn other traffic. If you have a vehicle, switch on your hazard warning lights. Stop anyone from smoking, and put on the gloves from your first-aid kit if you have one.

2. Get help

If you can do so safely, try to get the help of bystanders. Get someone to call the appropriate emergency services on 999 or 112 as soon as possible. They'll need to know the exact location of the incident (including the direction of traffic, for example, northbound) and the number of vehicles involved. Try to give information about the condition of any casualties, for example, if anyone is having difficulty breathing, is bleeding heavily, is trapped in a vehicle or doesn't respond when spoken to.

3. Help those involved

DO NOT move casualties from their vehicles unless there's the threat of further danger. DO NOT remove a motorcyclist's helmet unless it's essential. DO try to keep casualties warm, dry and as comfortable as you can. DO give reassurance confidently and try not to leave them alone or let them wander into the path of other traffic. DO NOT give them anything to eat or drink.

4. Provide emergency care

Remember the 'name' DR ABC (or Doctor ABC):

D – Danger: Check that it's safe to approach.

R – Response: Try to get a response by gently shaking the casualty's shoulders and asking loudly 'Are you all right?' If they respond, check for injuries.

A – Airway: If there's no response, open the casualty's airway by placing your fingers under their chin and lifting it forward.

B – Breathing: Check that the casualty is breathing normally. Look for chest movements, look and listen for breathing, and feel for breath on your cheek.

If there are no signs of breathing, start CPR. Interlock your fingers, place them in the centre of the casualty's chest and press down hard and fast – around 5 to 6 centimetres and about twice a second. You may only need one hand for a child and shouldn't press down as far. For infants, use two fingers in the middle of the chest and press down about a third of the chest depth. Don't stop until the casualty starts breathing again or a medical professional takes over.

C – Circulation: If the casualty is responsive and breathing, check for signs of bleeding. Protect yourself from exposure to blood and check for anything that may be in the wound, such as glass. Don't remove anything that's stuck in the wound. Taking care not to press on the object, build up padding on either side of the object. If nothing is embedded, apply firm pressure over the wound to stem the flow of blood. As soon as practical, fasten a pad to the wound with a bandage or length of cloth. Use the cleanest material available.

5. Burns

Put out any flames, taking care for your own safety. Cool the burn for at least 20 minutes with plenty of clean, cool water. Cover the burn with cling film if available. Don't try to remove anything that's sticking to the burn.

Be prepared

Always carry **a first aid kit** – you might never need it, but it could save a life. Learn first aid – you can get first aid training from a qualified organisation such as St John Ambulance (www.sja.org.uk), St Andrew's First Aid (www.firstaid.org.uk), British Red Cross (www.redcross.org.uk) or any suitable qualified body.

Safety advice: what to do if you break down

If you are on a non-motorway road

- Try to get your vehicle off the main road, or at least, get it right to the side of the road or on to the verge.

- If the vehicle is in a place where it might be hit by another vehicle, get any passengers out and to a safer place.

- Switch on the hazard warning lights to warn other drivers.

- If you have a red warning triangle, place it at least 45 metres behind your car to warn other traffic (but don't use it on a motorway).

- If you are a member of a breakdown organisation, call them and tell them where you are and what has happened. Wait with your vehicle until the patrol arrives.

If you are on a motorway

- If possible, leave the motorway at the next exit. If you can't get that far, drive on to the hard shoulder or, on a smart motorway, the next emergency refuge area. Stop far over to the left, with your wheels turned to the left, and switch on your hazard warning lights.

- Get everyone out of the vehicle, using the left-hand doors (leave animals in the vehicle unless they aren't safe there). Get them to sit on the bank, well away from the traffic.

- Use the nearest orange emergency phone to call the emergency services and tell them where you are and what has happened (for your safety, face the oncoming traffic while you are on the phone).

- Go back to your vehicle and wait on the bank near by until help arrives.

- Do *not:* cross the motorway on foot; or try to do repairs yourself – even changing a wheel. This is too dangerous on a motorway.

If you **can't get to a safe place** and you find yourself stuck in the middle or fast lane, then you should:

- stay in your vehicle

- keep your seatbelts and hazard warning lights on

- call 999 immediately and ask for the police.

Sample questions –
Incidents, accidents and emergencies

SAMPLE QUESTION 39

Which of the following is useful to carry in your car in case you have an accident?

Mark one answer

- ☐ **A** Can of fuel
- ☐ **B** Red warning triangle
- ☐ **C** Jump leads
- ☐ **D** Road atlas

Working out the answer to question 39

The question asks for those that are most useful if you are involved in an **accident**.

The red warning triangle is most useful in this situation because it can warn other drivers that a vehicle is causing a hazard.

But never place a warning triangle on a motorway.

So B is the right answer.

SAMPLE QUESTION 40

You are driving on a motorway. When are you allowed to switch on hazard warning lights?

Mark one answer

- ☐ **A** When towing another vehicle
- ☐ **B** When driving on the hard shoulder
- ☐ **C** On the hard shoulder, to warn others that you have broken down
- ☐ **D** When another vehicle is following you too closely

Working out the answer to question 40

The Highway Code does not say you should switch on hazard warning lights when towing. **Answer A** is therefore wrong.

As you know by now, the hard shoulder is only for use in an emergency, and you should not drive on it, so **answer B** is wrong.

If another vehicle is following you too closely you might need to slow down to leave a safer, bigger gap ahead. But you would not use your hazard warning lights in this situation. So **answer D** is wrong.

So C is the right answer.

SAMPLE QUESTION 41

You are at an accident scene and there is someone who is unconscious. Which should you check for urgently?

Mark one answer

- ☐ **A** Broken bones
- ☐ **B** Airway
- ☐ **C** Shock
- ☐ **D** If they are hungry

Working out the answer to question 41

Look back to the 'DR ABC of first aid' on pages 113, and you have the answer to this question: **Answer B** is the first part of Airway, Breathing and Circulation. Even if the casualty is conscious, you should never give them anything to eat or drink.

So B is the right answer.

14. VEHICLE LOADING

This last section, called Vehicle loading, is the shortest of all. It covers a mixture of the following:

- how to load your vehicle safely
- using a roof rack
- towing caravans and trailers
- child restraints and safety locks.

Q. Why do I need to learn the rules for towing?

- When you have passed your test you can tow a trailer, if the combined weight of the vehicle and trailer is less than 3,500kg. So you need to know the rules about towing.

Towing

When you get your first full driving licence, check it to see how much you are allowed to tow. **Do not tow any trailer that comes to more than that weight.**

The weight of a trailer should be no more than 85% of the weight of the car that is to pull it. But it is best to stay **well below** that top weight, because towing a trailer will **affect the way your vehicle handles.**

When you are towing, you need to allow:

- more room when **overtaking**

- more time to **brake and stop**.

When you are turning at a roundabout or junction you will need to think about where you are on the road.

Did you know?

A vehicle towing a trailer:

- must not go over a maximum speed limit of 60mph (see table on page 93)

- must not use the right (outside) lane on a motorway.

Roof racks

If you put a roof rack on your car, it will make a difference to the way your vehicle handles.

- The roof rack makes your vehicle taller, so more vulnerable to strong winds.

- You will increase your fuel consumption (use more fuel).

- You need to change the way you drive to allow for the extra weight.

Any load that is carried on a roof rack **must be tied down securely**.

To find out more, look up the parts of *The Highway Code* that deal with **Loads** and **Towing** (don't confuse 'Loads' with 'Loading and Unloading', which is about vehicles making deliveries).

When towing a heavy load, you might need to blow your tyres up to more than the normal pressures. Check your vehicle's handbook for advice. Remember to change back to the normal pressures when you finish your journey.

Loading a trailer

If the weight of the load is arranged properly, this should cut down the risk of **losing control, swerving and snaking** (see below).

- Try to **spread the weight evenly** when you load your trailer. Do not put more weight towards the front, or the back, or to one side.

- Remember – it is **against the law** to have a load that is **sticking out in a dangerous way**.

- Don't forget that if you park a vehicle with a trailer overnight, it must have **lights**.

Snaking

'Snaking' means moving from side to side. A caravan will snake if it is not properly attached or loaded, or if the car pulling it is going too fast.

Did you know?

If you are going to buy a trailer, make sure it fits your car's tow bar. Tow bars must keep to EU regulations, and must have electric sockets to connect to the lights on the trailer.

Vehicle loading

If you are towing a caravan or trailer and it starts to snake:

- slow down – stop pressing the accelerator (do not brake suddenly)
- get back in control of the steering
- then brake gently.

The driver's responsibility for the passengers

There are also questions in this section about the safety of passengers.

As the driver, you are responsible for **making sure your vehicle is not overloaded** – and this applies to **people and animals** as well as to luggage.

All passengers:

- must wear a **seat belt** (unless they have a medical certificate saying they should not wear one)
- all children under 14 must wear a seat belt or be strapped into a **child seat** or other 'restraint' suitable for their age. See the section on Child Restraints in *The Highway Code*.

Children must not sit in the **space behind the back seat** of a hatchback car, and no passengers should **sit in a caravan** while it is being towed.

Pets should be kept under careful control. You might keep them safe with a special harness, or behind a screen in a hatchback to stop them being thrown forward in an accident.

Sample questions – Vehicle loading

SAMPLE QUESTION 42

What should you do if the trailer you are towing starts to snake or swerve?

Mark one answer

- ☐ **A** Reduce speed by easing off the accelerator
- ☐ **B** Let go of the steering wheel so that the vehicle can correct itself
- ☐ **C** Speed up to drive out of the swerving
- ☐ **D** Brake hard and keep the brake pedal down

Working out the answer to question 42

Look back to the advice on snaking on pages 119–20. You should reduce speed – stop pressing the accelerator, as in **answer A**. To let go of the steering wheel (**Answer B**) would of course be extremely dangerous. Speeding up or braking hard (**C and D**) will both make the problem worse.

So A is the right answer.

SAMPLE QUESTION 43

Your passengers ask if they can ride in a caravan while you are towing it. Are they allowed to do this?

Mark one answer

- ☐ **A** Yes, if they are all over 14
- ☐ **B** Yes, if all the seats in the car are full
- ☐ **C** No, not at any time
- ☐ **D** Yes, as long as you are not on a motorway.

Working out the answer to question 43

You are responsible for seeing that all your passengers are safe. You must not let them ride in a towed caravan at any time.

So C is the right answer.

You should also check that all your passengers are wearing their seat belts, and that children are belted into child seats or child restraints.

SAMPLE QUESTION 44

You should not overload your vehicle as the excess weight will affect the

Mark one answer

- ☐ **A** battery
- ☐ **B** gearbox
- ☐ **C** journey time
- ☐ **D** steering

Working out the answer to question 44

You need to use some different driving skills when your vehicle is heavily loaded, when you have a roof rack fitted, or when you are towing a trailer. The vehicle may not respond as well as usual, and you might find that the steering feels different.

So D is the right answer.

Glossary

Accelerate
To make the vehicle move faster by pressing the right-hand pedal.

Adverse weather
Bad weather that makes driving difficult or dangerous.

Alert
Quick to notice possible hazards.

Anticipation
Looking out for hazards and taking action before a problem starts.

Anti-lock brakes
Brakes that stop the wheels locking so that you are less likely to skid on a slippery road.

Aquaplane
To slide out of control on a wet road surface.

Articulated vehicle
A long vehicle that is divided into two or more sections joined by cables.

Attitude
The way you think or feel, which affects the way you drive. Especially, whether you are patient and polite, or impatient and aggressive.

Automatic car
A vehicle with gears that change by themselves as you speed up or slow down.

Awareness
Taking notice of the road and traffic conditions around you at all times.

Blind spot
The section of road behind you which you cannot see in your mirrors. You cover your blind spot by looking over your shoulder before moving off or overtaking.

Brake fade
Loss of power to the brakes when you have been using them for a long time without taking your foot off the brake pedal. For example, when driving down a steep hill. The brakes will overheat and not work properly.

Braking distance
The distance you must allow to slow the vehicle in order to come to a stop.

Brow of a hill
The highest point of a hill.

Carriageway
One side of a road or motorway. A 'dual carriageway' has a central reservation.

Catalytic converter
A piece of equipment fitted in the exhaust system that changes harmful gases into less harmful ones.

Chicane
A sharp double bend that has been put into a road to make traffic slow down.

Child restraint
A child seat or special seat belt for children. It keeps them safe and stops them moving around in the car.

Clearway
A road where no stopping is allowed at any time. The sign for a clearway is a red cross in a red circle on a blue background.

Coasting
Letting the vehicle run down hill without using any of the gears. That is, with your foot on the clutch pedal or the car in neutral.

Commentary driving
Talking to yourself about what you see on the road ahead and what action you are going to take.

Glossary

Comprehensive insurance
A motor insurance policy that pays for all repairs even if you cause an accident.

Concentration
Keeping all your attention on your driving.

Conditions
How good or bad the road surface is, how much traffic is on the road, and what the weather is like.

Congestion
Heavy traffic that makes it difficult to get to where you want to go.

Consideration
Thinking about other road users and not just yourself. For example, letting another driver go first at a junction, or stopping at a zebra crossing to let pedestrians cross over.

Contraflow
When traffic on a motorway follows signs to move to the opposite carriageway for a short distance because of roadworks. (During a contraflow, there is traffic driving in both directions on the same side of the motorway.)

Coolant
Liquid in the radiator that removes heat from the engine.

Defensive driving
Driving safely without taking risks, looking out for hazards and thinking of others.

Disqualified
Stopped from doing something (eg driving) by law, because you have broken the law.

Distraction
Anything that stops you concentrating on your driving, such as chatting to passengers or on your mobile phone.

Document
An official paper or card, such as your driving licence.

Dual carriageway
A road or motorway with a central reservation.

Engine braking
Using the low gears to keep your speed down. For example, when you are driving down a steep hill and you want to stop the vehicle running away. Using the gears instead of braking will help to prevent brake fade.

Environment
The world around us and the air we breathe.

Equestrian crossing
An unusual kind of crossing. It has a button high up for horse riders to push.

Exhaust emissions
Gases that come out of the exhaust pipe to form part of the outside air.

Field of vision
How far you can see in front and around you when you are driving.

Ford
A place in a stream or river which is shallow enough to drive across with care.

Frustration
Feeling annoyed because you cannot drive as fast as you want to because of other drivers or heavy traffic.

Fuel consumption
The amount of fuel (petrol or diesel) that your vehicle uses. Different vehicles have different rates of consumption. Increased fuel consumption means using more fuel. Decreased fuel consumption means using less fuel.

Fuel gauge
A display or dial on the instrument panel that tells you how much fuel (petrol or diesel) you have left.

Gantry
An overhead platform like a high narrow bridge that displays electric signs on a motorway.

Handling
How well your vehicle moves when you steer or brake.

Harass
To drive in a way that makes other road users afraid.

Hard shoulder
The single lane to the left of the inside lane on a motorway, which is for emergency use only. You should not drive on the hard shoulder except in an emergency, or when there are signs telling you to use the hard shoulder because of roadworks.

Harsh braking (or harsh acceleration)
Using the brake or accelerator too hard so as to cause wear on the engine.

Hazard warning lights
Flashing amber lights which you should use only when you have broken down. On a motorway you can use them to warn other drivers behind of a hazard ahead.

High-sided vehicle
A van or truck with tall sides, or a tall trailer such as a caravan or horse-box, that is at risk of being blown off-course in strong winds.

Impatient
Not wanting to wait for pedestrians and other road users.

Inflate
To blow up – to put air in your tyres until they are at the right pressures.

Intimidate
To make someone feel afraid.

Involved
Being part of something. For example, being one of the drivers in an accident.

Jump leads
A pair of thick electric cables with clips at either end. You use it to charge a flat battery by connecting it to the live battery in another vehicle.

Junction
A place where two or more roads join.

Liability
Being legally responsible.

MOT
The test that proves your car is safe to drive. Your MOT certificate is one of the important documents for your vehicle.

Manoeuvre
Using the controls to make your car move in a particular direction. For example turning, reversing or parking.

Manual
By hand. So in a car that is a 'manual' or has manual gears, you have to change the gears yourself (see also Automatic car, on page 123).

Maximum
The largest possible; 'maximum speed' is the highest speed allowed.

Minimum
The smallest possible.

Mobility
The ability to move around easily.

Monotonous
Boring. For example, a long stretch of motorway with no variety and nothing interesting to see.

Motorway
A fast road that has two or more lanes on each side and a hard shoulder. Drivers must join or leave it on the left, via a motorway junction. Many kinds of slower vehicles – such as bicycles – are not allowed on motorways.

Glossary

Multiple-choice questions
Questions with several possible answers where you have to try to choose the right one.

Observation
The ability to notice important information, such as hazards developing ahead.

Obstruct
To get in the way of another road user.

Octagonal
Having eight sides.

Pedestrian
A person walking.

Pelican crossing
A crossing with traffic lights that pedestrians can use by pushing a button. Cars must give way to pedestrians on the crossing while the amber light is flashing. You must give pedestrians enough time to get to the other side of the road.

Perception
Seeing or noticing (as in hazard perception).

Peripheral vision
The area around the edges of your field of vision.

Positive attitude
Being sensible and obeying the law when you drive.

Practical Driving Test
The part of the test, taken in a vehicle, which is about driving skills.

Priority
The vehicle or other road user that is allowed by law to go first is the one that has priority.

Provisional licence
A first driving licence. All learner drivers must get one before they start having lessons.

Puffin crossing
A type of pedestrian crossing that does not have a flashing amber light phase.

Reaction time
The amount of time it takes you to see a hazard and decide what to do about it.

Red route
You see these in London and some other cities. Double red lines at the edge of the road tell you that you must not stop or park there at any time. Single red lines have notices with times when you must not stop or park. Some red routes have marked bays for either parking or loading at certain times.

Red warning triangle
An item of safety equipment to carry in your car in case you break down. You can place the triangle 45 metres before your car on the same side of the road. It warns traffic that your vehicle is causing an obstruction. (Do not use these on motorways.)

Residential areas
Areas of housing where people live. The speed limit is 30mph or sometimes 20mph.

Rumble strips
Raised strips across the road near a roundabout or junction that change the sound the tyres make on the road surface, warning drivers to slow down. They are also used on motorways to separate the main carriageway from the hard shoulder.

Safety margin
The amount of space you need to leave between your vehicle and the one in front so that you are not in danger of crashing into it if the driver slows down suddenly or stops. Safety margins have to be longer in wet or icy conditions.

Separation distance
The amount of space you need to leave between your vehicle and the one in front so that you are not in danger of crashing into it if the driver slows down suddenly or stops. The separation distance must be longer in wet or icy conditions.

Single carriageway
A road with no central reservation.

Snaking
Moving from side to side. This sometimes happens with caravans or trailers when you drive too fast, or they are not properly loaded.

Staggered junction
Where you drive across another road. Instead of going straight across, you have to go slightly to the right or left.

Sterile
Clean and free from bacteria.

Stopping distance
The time it takes for you to stop your vehicle – made up of 'thinking distance' and 'braking distance'.

Supervisor
Someone who sits in the passenger seat with a learner driver. They must be over 21 and have held a full driving licence for at least three years.

Tailgating
Driving too closely behind another vehicle – either to harass the driver in front or to make yourself feel safer in thick fog.

Thinking distance
The time it takes you to notice something and take the right action. You need to add thinking distance to your braking distance to make up your total stopping distance.

Third party insurance
A minimal insurance policy that will pay for damage to someone else's property if you have an accident.

Toucan crossing
A type of pedestrian crossing that does not have a flashing amber light phase. Cyclists are allowed to ride across.

Tow
To pull something behind your vehicle. It could be a caravan or trailer.

Traffic calming measures
Speed humps, chicanes and other devices placed in roads to slow traffic down.

Tread depth
The depth of the grooves in a car's tyres that help them grip the road surface. The grooves must all be at least 1.6mm deep.

Turbulence
Strong movement of air. For example, when a large vehicle passes a much smaller one.

Two-second rule
In traffic that's moving at any speed, allow at least a two-second gap between you and the vehicle in front.

Tyre pressures
The amount of air which must be pumped into a tyre in order for it to be correctly blown up.

Vehicle Excise Duty
The tax you pay for your vehicle so that you may drive it on public roads, also know as car tax.

Vehicle Registration Certificate
A record of details about a vehicle and its owner, also known as a 'log book'.

Vulnerable
At risk of harm or injury.

Waiting restrictions
Times when you may not park or load your vehicle in a particular area.

Wheel-spin
When the vehicle's wheels spin round out of control with no grip on the road surface.

Zebra crossing
A pedestrian crossing without traffic lights. It has an orange light, and is marked by black and white stripes on the road. Drivers must stop for pedestrians to cross.

Index

A
accidents 13, 24, 28, 29, 52, 64, 88, 92, 111–16
alertness 19–26, 51, 123
animals 66, 84, 87, 120
anticipation 20, 22, 29, 40, 44, 51, 57, 85, 123
attitude 22, 27–32, 45, 52, 123

B
blind spots 71, 85, 123
breakdown safety 114
brake fade 77, 80, 123
buses 55, 69, 72, 75–76, 89, 93

C
catalytic converter 37, 123
children 63–65, 120, 122
clearways 91, 94, 97–98, 102, 123
coasting 77, 80, 123
concentration 20, 24, 25, 30, 124
country roads 77, 79-80, 82, 92
cycle lanes 64, 71, 95
cyclists 30, 57, 58, 63, 64, 69, 70–71, 72, 73, 84

D
defensive driving 29, 124
disabled people 63, 67, 95
documents 105–110
driving lessons 5, 11, 14, 58, 83
driving licence 32, 105, 106, 108
dual carriageway 23, 57, 83, 98, 124

E/F
emergencies 111–16
engine braking 46, 77, 80, 124
First Aid 111, 112–13, 116
flashing lights 61, 84
fog lights 79, 82
fords 77, 80, 124
fuel consumption 118, 124

H
hard shoulder 84, 87, 88, 116, 125
hazard awareness 51–62
hazard perception element 6, 7–9, 13–18, 52
hazard warning lights 33, 34–35, 87, 111, 114, 115–16, 125

hazards 27, 44, 51, 53–56, 85, 86, 97, 115
hierarchy of road users 64
horn 68, 85

I/J/L
incidents 111–16
indicators 44, 60
instructor *see* driving lessons
insurance 105, 106, 110
junctions 55, 70, 71, 91, 94, 97, 118, 125
lane discipline 55, 57, 60, 70, 72, 83, 84, 85, 86, 88, 91
learner drivers 14, 63, 66, 83, 84, 105, 106, 108, 109–110
log book *see* Vehicle Registration Certificate
long vehicles 21–22, 42, 72, 75, 86

M
mirrors 20, 21, 25, 44, 56, 60, 71, 85
mobile phones 20, 24, 26, 30
MOT 105, 107, 109, 125
motorcycles 42, 63, 69, 71–72, 73, 74, 84, 89, 93
motorways 26, 35, 45, 47, 73, 82, 83–90, 94, 101, 114, 115–116, 118, 125

O/P
observation 20, 22, 57–59, 126
overtaking 30, 44, 77, 83, 85, 86, 89, 91, 97, 102, 118
parking 30, 34, 77, 91, 94–95, 96, 119
passengers 24, 30, 33, 36, 87, 114, 120, 121–22
pedestrian crossings 65, 91, 94
pedestrians 63, 64, 65–66, 67, 68, 76, 84, 97, 100, 126
Practical Driving Test 5, 65, 83, 100, 126

R
road markings 19, 23–24, 34, 51, 55, 91, 95, 100
road signs 19, 23, 51, 55, 57, 59, 60, 74, 84, 88, 91, 92, 99–104
road surface 48, 64, 77, 78, 80, 100

roadworks 44, 55, 88
roundabouts 55, 64, 70, 91, 118

S
safety 33–38, 111, 114
safety margins 39–50, 126
sample questions 21–26, 31–32, 34–37, 47–50, 60–62, 67–68, 74–76, 81–82, 88–90, 96–98, 102–104, 115–16
separation distances 39, 42–43, 81, 85, 86, 126
signalling 20, 64, 72, 75, 76, 85, 86
snaking 119, 121, 127
speed 29, 30, 32, 78, 83, 84, 89, 93
speed limits 28, 30, 45, 86, 88, 91, 92, 93, 97, 98, 118
stopping distances 38, 39, 41, 42, 43, 47, 127

T
towing 91, 93, 95, 98, 115, 116, 117, 118, 119, 120–22, 127
tractors 69, 73, 79, 84
traffic calming 77, 78, 81–82, 92, 127
traffic lights 51, 55, 57, 58, 100
traffic signs *see* road signs
trams 69, 72–73, 76, 78
two-second rule 40, 45, 50, 78, 81, 127
tyres 33, 35, 48, 84, 119

V
Vehicle Excise Duty 105, 107, 127
vehicle handling 48, 77–82, 83, 118, 122
Vehicle Registration Certificate 105, 108, 127
video test *see* hazard perception element
vulnerable road users 30, 42, 63–68, 127

W
weather conditions 45, 46, 77, 78–79, 80, 81, 88, 92, 93
wind 42, 64, 71, 74